Who's Driving the Bus?

Representative Diana S. Urban

Foreword by: Mark Friedman

Edited by: Olivier Kamanda

To my son, Lex Urban
and my Dad, Buzz Schwenk,
who have worked diligently to keep
my feet planted on Terra Firma.

A team of people made this possible and you meet them in the book. Three people you won't meet are Adam Luecking, former State Representative Steve Fontana, and Susan Scala. Adam, as CEO of Results Leadership Group, harassed and chased me, always with a great sense of humor, to finish this story...oh ya and he kind of supported me along the way. Steve was there when I said "did I really do this? Am I exaggerating?" to assure me I had it right and to push me to keep telling it like it is. And Susan shared her totally unique and artistic talent, sense of humor and wisdom to illustrate the book.

Table of Contents

Foreword

By Mark Friedman

Anyone telling you that they can solve all your budget problems with a bunch of formulas is selling you snake oil.

Budgeting is a political process, not a mathematical process. You have to exercise good judgment. And let's be honest, not everyone can do that. But if you use results-based methods, at least you'll have better budget choices, regardless of whether your budget expands or shrinks. Results Based Accountability™ (RBA) helps you focus on two basic questions to ask yourself about each program you're evaluating in the budget process:

1. Do we need it? (and assuming the answer is yes)

2. Is it working?

Using RBA, the first question can be answered in terms of population results. But we need to narrow the scope of this question a bit. In the context of population results, the question we're really asking is, "Do we need it because it is essential to improving the lives of our citizens?"

For many of you, you might be wondering "how do I define what's 'essential'?" If so, you're thinking too hard. The things that are essential are those which are necessary to reach your goals. If my goal is to build a house, land, lumber, and concrete are essential. A brand new high-definition TV, is not.

Similarly, we can determine whether something is "essential" for our community by analyzing the role the program plays in city, county, state or national quality of life.

Consider this: Every community wants "families that are strong and stable." But in order to achieve this, we need to have a number of building blocks in place. For example, among other things, we need absent fathers to pay child support. Unfortunately, many of these men will not do so unless forced, so that means we need a "Child Support Enforcement" program. Now that we've concluded that we need this program, we can evaluate it using data on its return on investment ("ROI"), i.e. child support dollars collected per dollar cost of the program.

Performance data can be used to answer the second question, "Is it working?" That data can help us make better decisions about use of funds because we can compare that data to other communities in our county and across the state. The performance data can show us quickly if we're doing better or worse. It can show us what options exist for improving the program when we have money to spend, or trimming the budget in a way that won't reduce the return on investment or weaken it with the impact on people's lives. And each time we use data to fine tune our Child Support Enforcement program, we come one step closer to stronger and more stable families.[1]

Here's another example: We all want "young people to succeed in school." And there's no shortage of ideas about how we can make that happen. Any active member of a PTA can rattle off a few: smaller class sizes, access to good teachers, the need to learn in a safe, comfortable environment. But we might also consider other factors that threaten this goal, like drug abuse. For years, Connecticut has funded Drug Abuse Resistence Education or "DARE," a local chapter of a national program founded in the 1980s to turn kids away from drugs, gangs, and violence. The anti-drug program had laudable goals and was well supported by school districts and police departments across the country.

Unfortunately, the performance data shows that DARE doesn't work. But don't just take my word for it. The U.S. Government Accountability Office[2] and the National Institutes of Health[3] said so, too. And now, no public school can spend federal money on DARE because the Department of Education found DARE ineffective in reducing alcohol and drug abuse. So this is a great example of how the performance data are screaming at us to cut the funding and put it to better use, but the political reality is much different. I can't imagine any freshman legislator wants to make a name for him or herself by cutting funds for drug abuse prevention in schools.

And therein lies the rub. At the end of the day, RBA can help you frame the decision and analyze the data, but you're the one who has to make the call and live with the political consequences. Would you take the heat for cutting a popular program, even if it doesn't work? Would you support a budget that forces agencies to do more with less? Are you willing to take the first step in tightening your own fiscal belt before you ask others to do so? These are the types of questions all legislators will have to wrestle with at some point in their career. And how you answer them will determine whether you're driving the legislative agenda or just going along for the ride.

One Legislator's Road to Results-Based Accountability

My name is Diana Urban and, if I had to guess, I'd say you're reading a book about results based budgeting to learn from my years of experience in the Connecticut State House of Representatives. That is why I have put my stories to paper, and I hope you find what I have to say in these pages both entertaining and informative.

But in the interest of full disclosure, the story you really want to hear—the one with all the practical lessons and pithy anecdotes—isn't really about the legislative process at all. It's about a question you will often hear when legislators are considering whether to support a particular bill: Who's driving the bus on this one? Let me explain . . .

In Connecticut, as in legislatures throughout the U.S., freshmen begin their terms full of exuberance and determination to change the world (or at least their little parts of it). Most, however, are quickly snapped back to reality and learn that real change comes hard to the public sector. Unfortunately, really great ideas about how to make government work better—including promises made during political campaigns—get the snot slapped out of them by tradition, entrenched power, institutional inertia and, of course, the insufferable legislative process. As the saying goes, "laws are like sausages, it is better not to see them made."

When I arrived in the Connecticut State House of Representatives in 2001, I too had a big agenda and full faith in my ability to execute it. In fact, I considered myself something of a Knightess of the Round Table with an electoral mandate to rebuild Camelot on the eastern seaboard, beginning with the battle of Hartford! Not surprisingly, I took quite a few hard knocks as I tried to move my agenda. And like all bright-eyed, bushy-tailed freshmen before and since, I spent countless hours lamenting the political, institutional, and budgetary barriers that seemed to stymie what I wanted to accomplish on behalf of Connecticut's citizenry at every turn.

I'll let you in on a poorly-kept secret: our federal, state, and local governments are broken (in fact, broke). As a result, it's hard to make meaningful headway through the legislative processes. Start a conversation about politics at your local coffee shop or turn on cable news and inevitably that's the message you're going to hear. There are plenty of reasons things are the way they are (too many to bore you with here) and lots of reasons why changing those conditions can be damn near impossible (ditto). But the fact that our governments are often supremely screwed up, or that you're going to catch hell for challenging the establishment, is hardly an excuse to accept the status quo. At least it's not for me.

So early in my tenure I had a choice: ride the bus along the current route or take the wheel, inspire people to join me, and drive the bus on the road to accountability and transparency. I decided on the latter and staked my political capital on an effort to increase the efficiency and effectiveness of Connecticut's budgeting processes. As in most states, Connecticut's budget was typically constructed around prior program investments, solutions *du jour*, aka pet projects, and hasty responses to whatever crises were then being precipitated by long-ago policy mistakes. I actually refer to this as incremental budgeting. You want to know why our budgets just seem to grow and grow? Simple. We pass what we consider to be great programs, they become a part of the budget base, and we go on our merry way never following up to see if those programs are actually working.

To be fair, there is plenty of other stuff on the agenda keeping us busy. There always seems to be a new crisis—in health care, energy, pensions— and we just hope that while we're navigating through the storm, the bus isn't careening off the road or taking an entirely different road than we envisioned. In fact, there are programs in the budget base that have become a giant black hole. We have no idea what or how they are doing. Some have been there languishing in the great budget abyss since I was a kid.

So each year we start with a budget base, but we have no idea what's in it. Then, we add new programs. The cycle continues and rarely is any type of performance or outcome data used to determine if these new investments did a lick of good. And each year the older programs become more heavily fortified within that budget base.

This way of budgeting favors both the status quo (i.e., "let's keep doing what we always did") and the reactionary (i.e., "let's undo all the damage the last guys did"). It also tends to throw good money after bad. I found this maddening and unacceptable. There had to be a better way to bring the benefits of a performance-based framework to Connecticut's public sector and hold government accountable for the outcomes of budget decisions.

That's why in 2005, I introduced a bill to bring performance-based budgeting to the state of Connecticut. Actually, I re-introduced a bill that we had passed in 1992 but were ignoring. Yup, you read that right. We had a law on the books mandating that Connecticut incorporate performance budgeting into the budget process, and for years the legislature just ignored it. "Performance-" or "results-based" budgeting are the technical names for a data-driven budgeting process that allocates resources to accomplish specific outcomes, with a clear and transparent feedback loop. In most iterations, this type of budgeting is not a walk in the park. So instead of tackling something that is quite difficult, we stumble from various budgeting models and reporting formats with no consistency of purpose, sometimes at the behest of the executive branch, other times at the behest of the legislature.

As I remember seeing it, I had two options: reintroduce the bill or sue my own colleagues for not following the laws they passed. The latter did not seem to be the best way to win friends in the legislature. So, I changed a few words and put it back on the House floor.

Curiously, no one seemed concerned that the state was out of compliance with its own statute or that the relationship between spending and accountability for outcomes was anything but clear. I wanted to change things on both fronts. And I thought that with some clever reframing and just a little bit of cajoling, I could get the job done quickly and relatively painlessly.

I was wrong. Nothing about the process was easy. The executive branch, legislature, and state agencies were not necessarily opposed to performance-based budgeting, but it was a foreign concept and they were busy (as they endemically are). In the absence of a central authority or charismatic champion telling them what to do or how to do it, incentives to pursue and sustain meaningful changes in state budgeting procedures were few and far between, and the status quo (i.e., comfortable, traditional, and even "cover your ass" practices) largely held fast. So, for a long time it was practically impossible to track the real return and impact of spending on agency or program performances and population outcomes.

But I am nothing if not persistent—or as I often say I have the world's flattest learning curve! If you want to shape budgetary priorities for the greater good, you simply have to be willing to hit the wall repeatedly, bounce off and find another way around. And when you hit that wall, you need friends who will pick you up, dust you off and say, "Wow, nice hit. How ya doin'?" Were it not for the people who decided that this battle was worth it, and that I was crazy enough and tenacious enough to not let go, I never would have succeeded.

This book tells the story of the group of tenacious Connecticut legislators and dedicated staff people who successfully piloted and scaled (with only minimal kicking and screaming!) a results-informed budgeting process and the important lessons they learned about design and implementation along the way. Although I believe our legislature's experience and lessons-learned are broadly applicable to other legislative bodies, this is not meant to be a "how to" guide *per se*. Rather, it is meant to serve as inspiration and a call to action for legislators who want to find a way not to merely ride the bus, but to drive the bus and steer public budgeting processes to increase transparency, drive continuous improvement initiatives and, ultimately, increase the wellbeing of citizens.

I Get By with a Little Help from My Friends

Here's the first big lesson for all you newly-minted legislators: no matter how confident you are that you can do this job by yourself, you are totally wrong. The Beatles got it right. Not only will you need help from your friends to get by, you'll have to venture outside of your comfort zone to find new friends, too.

Why is this the fundamental lesson of this chapter? Because you have to decide where the bus is going before you start driving it, and you can't do that alone. Consider this: well before you consider what goes into your budget, you need to determine whether you even have the right *strategy* for budgeting. How will you decide which of the many strategies to choose from? Should you adopt "performance-based" budgeting or "planned programming" budgeting? Are your communities better served by "budgeting for outcomes," "zero-based" budgeting, or as one of my mentors used to say "bouillabaisse" budgeting?

Sorry, you can't look to the feds for guidance. When stories surfaced about $600 toilet seats and $9,000 wrenches at the Department of Defense, we started to realize that our federal cabinet agencies haven't mastered the budget process either.

Trying to figure all of this out by yourself would drive you mad. Believe me, I have been there. And I even taught this stuff! This is no college final exam where you cram the night before and make brilliant observations the next day. It didn't work then, and it certainly isn't going to work now!

So how do we expect our legislators, many of whom are part-time, who range from Ph.D.'s to "no-degrees" (although way too many JDs) to study all these iterations of bliss in budgets?

You need to find out what is going on right now in your state's budget process. And this is a little harder than it seems. I bet that if you were to ask five legislators the same question about budget priorities you would get five different answers with varying degrees of applicability. To further complicate the issue, every response will be shaded by the particular perspective, political agenda, geographic representation, and leadership rank of the legislator. What to do?

Step 1. Find a budget guru. That's what I did, and I highly recommend it. Find the person who sits in on negotiations, who sets up appropriations meetings, informational hearings, and anything else that needs to be done to get vital information to the legislature. In short, find the person whose job it is to get the bus started.

In Connecticut, that person is the Administrator of the Appropriations Committee, Susan Keane, and she has been working in state government for thirty years. As you can imagine, she knows every nook and cranny of the capitol down to where the mice are hiding and chewing on the wires in the bus' engine. Do whatever it takes to find that person.

To say I surprised her with my request to be "schooled" on the budget process would be an understatement. It is not the norm for legislators to wander into an administrator's office looking to become a student. Breaking that silly barrier allowed us to get places not normally visited. In the process we became fast friends, and I had a person always watching my back. The RBA journey never would have started if I hadn't approached her with my usual goofy smile and asked her to teach me. She was willing to share her vast knowledge of the ins and outs of the budget process and made it possible for us to have a fighting chance to get this accountability tool moving.

Your first conversation with your budget guru will enlighten you. So don't forget to bring a notebook. You will learn things you thought you already knew as well as things you never knew that you never knew (ask Donald Rumsfeld about that one). And as your awareness of worlds unknown expands, your ego will just as quickly contract. So go ahead and put your ego to bed now.

Step 2. Find state people with experience. Remember, just because you are the "omniscient" legislator (or at least think you are after all the attention that follows winning an election) that doesn't mean that you can't learn from staff. They have been down this road many times before watching the legislative bus careen around blind corners as if it had no driver, then recover direction and speed, and once again swerve out of control with each new legislative session. Imagine their frustration as the hours they sacrifice towards an initiative pile up, only to see that same project crash and burn into the great legislative abyss.

No matter what state you're in, there are staff people that have years of experience under their belt who can keep you from making the same errors as your predecessors. And make room on the bus for the up-and-coming young whippersnappers fresh from college with boundless energy and novel ideas. Don't be afraid of them. They want to change the world! So engage them and show them that you are in it for the long haul.

Now that you have your budget guru, experienced staff, and fresh eager-beavers, you should be ready to take off, right?

Step 3. Find good consultants. If you're serving in a part-time legislature, as most are, you'll want to find a consultant to work with you. Your consultants should be dedicated to public service, be willing to work crazy hours, and not blow you off when you tell them, "This report is too long, too complex, there's no way a legislator will take the time to read it!" Consultants have a tendency to make the simple much more complex, so you have to find one willing to be schooled by a pain-in-the-butt legislator and a maven of appropriations. And they have to be cheap. Not easy, but totally worth the search! We were fortunate to find the Charter Oak Group and in particular, Bennett Pudlin, who shared our passion to uproot an entrenched budget system.

Step 4. Find allies and collaborators. You will also need to find legislative allies with strong budget backgrounds and a reputation for fearlessness. You want to find people with strength of character who aren't afraid to make tough decisions if they believe those are the right decisions.

If you're lucky, you may stumble upon your legislative ally through no deliberate action of your own. I found my first ally through a scheduling snafu at the National Conference of State Legislators (NCSL). Right before the conference began, I got word that Denise Merrill, House Chair of Appropriations, couldn't get a room at the host hotel. We knew each other before but this sealed the deal. We had similar frustrations with the budget process and were willing to work together for change. I offered to share my hotel room. We also happened to both be musicians, but she went on to study law, and I went on to study economics. I'm not sure I would always recommend that combo, but it worked for us!

My second ally came along a bit later. He also filled an essential role that I call "The Enforcer," but more about him in a bit.

At the time, NCSL was experimenting with various budgeting methodologies and trying to solve the eternal budgeting puzzle. The NCSL leadership approached Denise and me about something called "Results-Based Accountability" (RBA) with a book titled, *Trying Hard Isn't Good Enough*. Catchy.

What we both appreciated was that RBA is a system that everyone could understand. You don't need a degree in public policy, finance, or management to get it. In fact, one of the basic tenets of RBA is to express all ideas in words that the average Joe or Jane can understand. Everything's spelled out so no one is excluded.

Here's why that matters: I was chairing a lively discussion at an RBA Jobs Summit, and I asked a commissioner on the panel, "So do you think that you can improve the ROI without increasing costs and still stay within your budget?" We launched into an even more involved conversation about the ins and outs of ROI, until I realized that people in the meeting didn't know what the hell we were talking about.

Most people are too embarrassed to ask for the definition of a word or acronym if they think everyone else knows what it means. When that happens, they become less likely to play an active role in the conversation. That's the last thing we want. So, as a perfect example of why we use words that everyone can understand, I looked at the camera and said, "for those of you who are wondering, ROI stands for return on investment—how much bang for our buck."

Denise and I were sold on RBA. We then convinced the House leadership that RBA was important enough to warrant the creation of a subcommittee of our Appropriations Committee. We knew we had two really good arguments. If the House leadership couldn't see the *policy* value of a tool that can help identify which programs and agencies were working for the people of Connecticut, then we would appeal to the *political* value of the tool. If you were a legislator facing re-election, would you want to appear like you had been sitting on your hands while the deficit grew out of control or would you want to be able to say you actually supported a framework to bring accountability and transparency to government?

I know. I know. That might sound a little cynical, but sometimes you have to do whatever it takes to get the job done! Or in RBA terms, focus on the end and work backwards to the means.

And guess what? It worked. Not only did we establish an RBA subcommittee within the Appropriations Committee, we even recruited some analysts from our non-partisan Office of Fiscal Analysis to shield it from pure party politics.

And now, the last step.

Step 4. Find an enforcer. When the House Appropriations co-Chairs told us we needed a Senate co-Chair of our subcommittee, I knew we needed someone that was not afraid to cut to the chase. We needed someone who would eschew superfluous niceties in favor of a plain direct approach. He or she also needed to have experience promoting accountability. Luckily, Bob Duff, a senator from Norwalk immediately came to mind. I had worked on a bill with him on the funding of our Department of Agriculture spay/neuter program and had been very impressed. Here's what happened:

I was having a problem with Representative Julia Wasserman, a smart, venerable, and respected legislator from across the aisle. We simply could not agree on the language for the bill and had come to an impasse. Senator Duff was also interested in the bill so we set up a meeting with Representative Wasserman. I prepared by gathering statistics, putting together an irrefutable economic argument and just generally getting myself in a tizzy. After all, Julia was superbly educated, and I would have to bring my A-game. So there we were sitting in the conference room while I waxed poetic, and Julia kept slamming my words back at me. To make matters worse, my supposed ally Bob was busy checking his emails, while I was hashing it out with Julia.

After a while I ran out of stuff to say because we were clearly at an impasse. And then, Bob surprised all of us. He looked up from his Blackberry, said what was on all of our minds: Julia really didn't like the bill. He then ripped the bill in half and threw it in the trash.

WHAT????? That was my bill!!! It is hard to render me speechless, and both Julia and I were at a loss for words.

Bob then pulled out a blank sheet of paper and said, "Let's see where we can agree" and in less than half an hour we had a bill that we could all support and I finally found my "Enforcer."

None of this would have happened without the friends I made along the way. The budget guru. The staffers. The consultants. The legislative allies. Everyone played a part in getting the bus rolling. And I have no doubt, you'll have a similar experience. But you have to be a cheerleader who believes in making a difference if you want to go down this path. The team we were building was coming together for all the right reasons even if sometimes we had to sell it for all the wrong (political) reasons. That commitment to common cause was essential, and the friendships we formed gave us a boost in times of trial, made us laugh together in time of legislative ridiculousness, and gave the finish line new meaning as we took each step towards a true RBA system.

And I never discount luck. When Denise moved on to become Secretary of State, the new House Chair, John Geragosian was equally supportive. He then moved on to become the State Auditor (do I see a trend here?). His successor was State Representative Toni Walker from New Haven who was doing amazing work on juvenile justice. Talk about a gift to RBA! She was a one-woman army for juvenile justice accountability and programs that work. Representative Walker had led the fight on a "Raise the Age" campaign to increase the age at which children may be prosecuted as adults. She used a data-based approach to counter arguments that this would increase the numbers in our juvenile justice system and cost a lot of money. She stuck to the data and was proven right and thereby made troubled youth in our state enormously better off. My kind of gal!

But, I'm not going to sugar coat it. This was no walk in the park. And that brings us to the next chapter, where I discuss the pitfalls to avoid. I can't even count the number of times we went down the rabbit hole and had to find our way out again. As enticing as it may seem, if you look down that rabbit hole, you'll find yourself in a maze of individual legislative priorities. In a way, it reminds me of *Alice in Wonderland* when the Cheshire Cat observes that if you don't know where you are going, it doesn't matter what road you take.

If you do know where you want to lead, RBA can put you on the road to results. Now, all you have to do is herd all those legislative "Cheshire Cats" onto the bus—the Government Accountability Bus or "GAB" as it is so well-known!

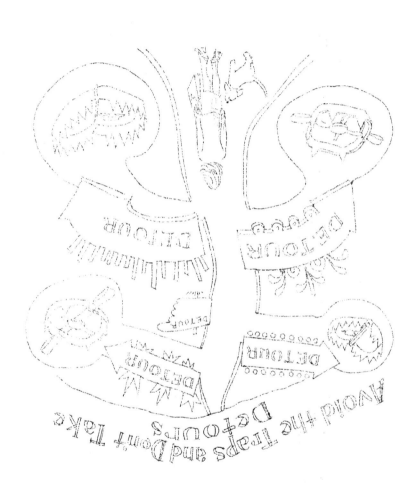

3

Avoid the Traps and Don't Take Detours

Top Five Common Traps for Legislatures Implementing Results-Based Accountability and Strategies to Overcome Them

RBA is a process. And like any other process, there are guideposts that can keep you on track and pitfalls that can derail your progress. In Connecticut and throughout the country, I have advised state legislators on both. Below, based on my experience working with others on RBA, I have identified the five most common traps as well as strategies to avoid them:

#1 - The "Failure to Follow Up" Trap

You understand the value of RBA. In fact, you may be one of many legislators who want to adopt RBA. Good for you! Now get ready to carry the mantle. Because even if the entire legislature wanted to implement RBA, you still aren't done making the case for it. You need buy-in from other branches and agencies as well. Too often, the agencies responsible for implementing the programs or launching the initiatives are left out of the discussion about RBA. As a result, budget plans or fixes are inconsistent and may even be in conflict with what the legislature has proposed.

RBA works best when all the affiliated and affected agencies over which you have oversight are willing to sign on to the plan too. A proposal without the buy-in from people working to make it reality is just another piece of paper. And there is way too much paper floating around the statehouse already. So those responsible for managing the budget process, have to explain to all stakeholders not only what RBA *can* do, but also anticipate what RBA *should* do. That means starting with a clear understanding of the end-goals—what we're calling the *Population Results*. By following up with representatives of state agencies, you can share the *Population Result* as it relates to each agency.

For example, one *Population Result* from Connecticut was "A Healthy and Productive Long Island Sound for Connecticut Residents." So it made sense for the legislature to approach the Department of Environmental Protection, given their role in implementing programs that would affect this particular *Population Result*. Once the agencies and other stakeholders are on board with the end-goal, the next step is to use RBA to work backwards to identify the means.

Another example is Nurturing Families, a program spanning twenty-nine birthing hospitals in Connecticut that provides assistance to first-time parents who might need a little extra help with their new responsibilities. It aims to reduce child abuse and promote positive parenting by keeping children healthy, developmentally on track, and ready to learn. Sounds good, right? Well, before RBA the program was shuffled around, put on the chopping block, left out in the cold, and forced to scramble every year to survive. It wasn't until one of our official "Legislators-Get-Off-Their-Asses-And-Visit-An-Agency" days, that the agency committed to keeping the program and updating a RBA Report Card.

Now, fast-forward to the next budget cycle. The data from the RBA Report Card not only empowered us to keep the program from getting cut several times, but it prompted us to expand its operations and bring the program to scale. Without RBA and the cooperation of the program director, Nurturing Families may have gotten the axe when we fell into the Great Recession, just as the need for this type of program was growing.

But instead, whenever it came up to our committee as a candidate for the cutting board, I would direct the committee's attention to the RBA Report Card that showed falling child abuse rates, increasing participant level of education, and growing employment rates of parents.

That's what you can do when a program is working. If you can prove it, it gets funded. Bingo!

But it can't end there. After all, this is titled the "Failure to Follow Up Trap," right? You have to keep the focus on the RBA Report Card. Bring it up in any meeting to illustrate that it is useful to the agency. Bring it up with legislators, so they know to look for the data. In discussions with the Nurturing Families program director, Karen Foley-Schain,we learned that she felt that it was a great relief to finally use data in a constructive way, knowing that the legislature would pay attention. It's not an easy solution, but it's a simple one. And if you start off on the right foot, the rest of this work becomes much more manageable.

#2 - The "WeBe" Trap

State legislators come and go each election cycle. And nearly every class of new legislators yields some new plan to redo the budget and undo the damage done by the last class of legislators (no hard feelings, that's just how the game is played). The state agencies have heard it all before. They have learned to tune out the song and dance and do what they've always done because that's how it's always been done. The easiest thing for the agency staff to do is maintain the status quo, resulting in the "We Be Here When You Gone" (WeBe) trap. This is just another iteration of the "budget *de jour*" where agencies assume that legislators will lose interest in their new flavor-of-the-month methodology.

Don't let that happen. If agency staff or other legislators believe they can wait you out, you won't get the buy-in that you need. If they believe that all they need to do is prep for that first big high-profile budget meeting and go back to business as usual the next day, you haven't done your job.

To head these types of problems off, you and your fellow legislators need to communicate consistently and in a bipartisan manner. In Connecticut, we did so by assigning legislators who were members of the Appropriations RBA subcommittee to affiliated agencies. Each subcommittee member had to visit the agencies on his or her own turf (this also helps with the "Gotcha" trap that I explain next).

But the responsibility doesn't solely lie with the legislators either. You have to get each agency director to delegate officially and unequivocally a key RBA person involved at every meeting. This is not so easy. When you bring this up, often the agencies hear, "this is extra work." What you want them to hear is, "this is the way to the appropriations committee's heart." Once they understand that, they'll start to appreciate how useful RBA can be.

One of our biggest breakthroughs was after addressing a $20 million problem explained further in the "Gotcha" trap with our Department of Education. We watched as the agency transformed itself into an "RBA Thinking Group." A deputy commissioner was assigned as the RBA lead and the tenets of RBA became part of their roundtable discussions. They even established recognition awards for implementing RBA. This was another opportunity for us to show up at the agency and attend those recognition awards. Was the staff surprised? Absolutely!

Our Department of Energy and Environment Commissioner at the time, Gina McCarthy, who was later asked to join the Obama Administration was another amazing partner. All she could talk about was how important the data is to making decisions and how committed she was to the process. Finding a commissioner like her really helps move the ball along. We will revisit her in the "Too Much Too Soon" trap.

Remember, the goal here is a "culture change." If someone isn't complaining that, "this isn't how we used to do it" or, "we've always done it the other way" then you're doing something wrong. You, the other legislators, and agency representatives need to make it known that you're interested in effective change.

Work towards having a full-time, dedicated analytic staff (this took us three years) and be sure to keep "Questions for the Record" so you don't keep revisiting the same territory (legislators tend to forget the questions that they ask in committee meetings!). You need to be clear about what results you are trying to produce, who is responsible, what success would look like, and how we know if we are making improvements.

Legislators tend to believe that all they need to do is pass a law or deliver a speech about some profound topic and like magic, "things will happen." The hungry will be fed. The children will be taught. The poor will be employed. We can actually picture the bus following just the right route, at just the right speed, making just the right turns, and when it arrives, we can finally take that much-deserved vacation.

If only!

The reality is that legislators need to get taken out of their comfort zones. Too often, a legislator complains about a problem, and a low-level staffer is sent by an agency to put the fire out. So, we decided it was time for our subcommittee members to meet the agencies on their own turf. We split up the committee and sent them to the agencies to discuss RBA and the programs we wanted to learn about.

I remember the first expedition I went on. In fact, I will probably never forget how awkward the commissioner and his staff were when we greeted them. I could tell they were on high alert. What were we up to? Why did we want to talk to them now? Whose job is on the chopping block?

After we broke the ice, things got better. It was an enlightening conversation for both sides. The best part was that when the commissioners and their staff came to see us for their appropriations meetings, there was a level of familiarity that made a discussion of data constructive rather than confrontational. We had gone the extra mile to let the agencies know this wasn't the latest budgeting fad. It was a new way of approaching accountability and transparency, and we were serious about it.

As one of my favorite commissioners, Joette Katz, put it, "RBA can be a sword or a shield." Coming from our Department of Children and Families (DCF), I know that was a mouthful. I bet her team was thinking in the shield mode as she continued, "when we find programs that don't work and yet we know that they might be some legislator's priority that is when RBA becomes a sword for accountability." And of course she is right on. Accountability must involve the legislative as well as the executive.

#3 - The "Gotcha" Trap

No one wants to be the poster child for budget overruns and low productivity. The "Gotcha" trap is created when agencies feel like they are being singled out (always unfairly in their mind) and made an example of poor performance. It presents a risk of passing on a real opportunity to improve results. In the best case scenario (if they don't believe you really care), this can be seen as a slap on the wrist and you lose credibility. But in the worst-case scenario, they may feel like victims of an outright attack. Either case creates a bad public relations environment, a missed opportunity for collaboration, and a mental footnote to never willingly work with you again.

Be tactful when handling agencies or programs that need budget discipline. Constructive criticism lies somewhere between derisive commentary and boring lecturing. You need to find the right balance between the brutal and the bland. If you're too critical you risk managers saying,

"What a cool hammer!" and then go looking for some nails to pound. If you're too bland you end up sounding like a fifth grade "show and tell" presentation.

Insist on data, but don't rely on brutal censure without offering an opportunity to improve and earn compliments. Just because a program isn't working at top efficiency doesn't mean it's ready for the chopping block. Use the evidence you have to make the case for *how* the program might improve. We cut $20 million from an Early Reading Success program and ended up with incredible dialogue because we opened the doors for communication and did not turn it into a "Gotcha" trap.

Early Reading Success

With all the consequences of illiteracy—from dependence on welfare to growing prison rolls, who in their right mind would oppose an Early Reading Success program? It seems like a no-brainer, right? Well, that assumes that Early Reading Success was actually a successful program!

Whenever the Appropriations Committee asked the typical questions about the status of the program, we'd get the typical agency answer, "Things are great, but they would be better if you gave us more money." After a few rounds of that song and dance, we started digging a bit deeper. We found that reading scores were actually *falling* in our priority school districts. So when the budget cycle came up around again and we were considering another multi-million investment, we had a choice. We could have used this as a "Gotcha" moment or as a moment of opportunity.

It would have been really easy to single out the bad schools and bad teachers, cut their funding, and move on to the next budget item. But if we'd done that we never would have moved passed the symptoms (falling test scores) and diagnosed the problem (the reason scores were falling despite ample spending on reading).

And who better to break down the problem? The RBA subcommittee—here to save the day with pesky questions about efficacy. But we actually wanted the data. As we drilled down into the program, we asked the three simple RBA foundational questions: How much are you doing? How well are you doing it? Is anyone better off?

The answers started trickling in. Then we invited the State Department of Education to work *with* us. We made it clear that we weren't interested in a "Gotcha" but really wanted to figure out what was going on. We weren't going to hold primetime press conferences or set anybody up as a fall guy. And soon folks at the agency started to tell us the background story that explained the trends in the data, aka the "story behind the curve."

It turns out that money was mostly being spent on almost everything *but* improving children's reading. With no strings attached to the money, our priority school districts were directing significant funds to all-day kindergarten (a worthy goal but not part of this mission), playgrounds, and other facilities. Don't get me wrong. Jungle gyms are great, but they aren't going to help little Timmy with his ABCs.

We also found that 9 out of 10 teachers had no specific academic background in teaching reading. When other teachers were brought into the classroom to coach, there wasn't any training requirement for them either! Instead, coaches were chosen by the principal for reasons that—under scrutiny—were unclear at best. As you can imagine, each year things got a little worse than the year before— a dangerous consequence of incremental budgeting.

With no one asking the tough questions, programs continue to grow even though they weren't working!

But here's the good news. Once the commissioner's eyes were opened to the problem, he became a proponent of RBA and a willing partner. Instead of avoiding engaging with the legislature for fear of the "Gotcha" trap we were able to forge a relationship based on mutual interest.

In the end, we actually did cut funds for Early Reading Success. And if you don't think that was tough, think again. In the run-up to our decision, we could picture the headline, "Committee Cuts Funds For Early Reading Success" marking the end of our careers in the legislature. I actually had one of my favorite senators come to me and say—actually it was more of a shout, "How can you cuts these funds? Are you crazy?!?"

It took a little while, but I showed her the data and the trends that shaped our decision. She gasped. I explained that we could keep the funding and watch reading scores continue to fall or cut the funds and fine tune the programs until they worked. Finally, she saw the light. Cutting the funding to the program isn't the point. The point is to put the money where it works!

And the data did show one school district program that had succeeded in improving reading scores (and it was in Senator Duff's district, what a surprise!). The State Department of Education is even using it as a model for other school districts. Our committee also requested an increase in the reading course requirements for a Connecticut teaching certificate by attaching strings to any future state funding. The school districts in question stepped up to the plate and found money in their budgets to institute changes. When an open dialogue began between the Appropriations Committee, the State Department of Education, and the school districts directed at making Connecticut children better off, we saw it as an example of RBA at its best. And as a result, our latest Children's Report Card shows improvement in our third grade reading scores from 52.1% to 56.9% from 2008 to 2013.

#4 - The "Language" Trap

If you have come this far in the book it is a safe assumption that you understand English. Although we share a language, we may have different understanding of syntax, spelling, grammar, and vocabulary. As the reader, if something I've written doesn't make sense or confuses you, you have options. You can re-read a section, look up a word in the dictionary, or skip the offending phrase altogether and try to understand my meaning from the context.

But if you're attending a meeting or live presentation, you don't have a second chance to resolve a misunderstanding. And the only thing worse than trying to engage in a discussion with others who use words you don't understand, is when others use words you *think* you understand.

Words like "goal," "outcome," or "benchmark," are common terms with which most people are familiar. But the words have very specific definitions within the RBA framework. Given that most people aren't familiar with RBA, they won't understand what you mean at first and no one will interrupt you to ask you to explain the "goal." As the discussion continues, your audience will begin using these and other key words interchangeably, threatening any chance of meaningful discourse as no one is sure what the heck you are really talking about as terms are being used interchangeably. Once that happens, it will be almost impossible to get everyone back on track.

Legislators, legislative staff, and agency heads need to speak the same language so they don't speak past each other. The best way to ensure that is to prepare a primer or glossary of RBA and budget-related terms. It doesn't take a lot of time to do, but by agreeing upon the use of terms in advance you will be better able to express ideas and establish a meaningful dialogue.

One of our venerable state senators, Edith Prague, is a staunch fan of RBA and a veritable legend in the Senate for the work she does for children and the aging—someone you absolutely need on your side. But she also had a tendancy to substitute any word she didn't like with one she preferred and assumed that we would just fill in the blanks and understand what she was talking about. The problem is that when you are trying to establish a dialogue with an agency, word choice can be crucial. Are we talking about a "goal" or a "benchmark"? Or perhaps an "outcome"? And what do we mean by the word we choose?

In our Appropriations Committee implementation of RBA we chose to use "result," but that didn't stop her one bit, until we made her the "chief RBA interrogator" on her favorite labor programs. She spent a significant amount of time reviewing the report cards on labor programs and during the review she eventually appreciated why it was so important that everyone speak the same language. She looked at me and asked why didn't I just tell her it was confusing if different people used different words? I bit my tongue and didn't remind her that we had the RBA glossary so that we could all speak the same language. After all, getting her to agree to take the lead role in questioning worked pretty well, so who am I to complain?

But you won't always be so lucky. So help all parties involved appreciate the importance of a common language, and stick to using the terms as they're used in the glossary!

#5 - The "Too Much, Too Soon" Trap

RBA is like a Swiss Army knife. It has a lot of tools for a lot of situations. From performance management to program management, delegation to decision-making, RBA can be applied to solve many different challenges. But it can't solve every problem overnight. Just like a Swiss Army knife won't help you build a bridge or fly an airplane, RBA has its limits too.

Those who are familiar with RBA understand its benefits, but they may not fully appreciate its limits. The "Too Much, Too Soon" trap refers to instances when a legislator or agency director decides that after a few quick successes, RBA should be adopted immediately, across the board.

The big, institutional changes, like the need for accountability or governmental reform, take time. When leadership attempts to rush this process, they do everyone a disservice. Start with one well-defined result area, pilot it, get buy-in, get your problem solved, and then move on to the next one. You don't have to do it all at once. The key is to *slow down in order to speed up the pace of change.*

One of our first *Results Statements* was "A Clean and Healthy Long Island Sound" and our Department of Environmental Protection (DEP) Commissioner Gina McCarthy, at that time was a data person extraordinaire. She had a knack for numbers, knew how to mine the data, and to top it all off, she had an endless enthusiasm for the process.

She had measures all over the place and tons of places to drill down. We spent some time trying to find a focused place to succeed and make a measurable improvement. We knew that stationary sewage treatment plants were effective, but they were expensive and nitrogen was still contaminating the Long Island Sound. Could we find a new, cheaper solution to this challenge? We wanted to encourage the agency to be creative, engage the public and the legislature and not immediately jump to the more money for stationary plants solution. So we set up brainstorming sessions with DEP staff and legislators, asking them what would they do if they had no money and what would they do if they had unlimited funds. The idea was to get the dialogue started. Working in teams brought about some hilarious proposals for what to do with all the money in the world. One I remember was a proposal for a giant version of the Roomba vacuum cleaner that would zoom around the Long Island Sound sucking up sewage. The image still makes me laugh!

It also worked to inspire some really creative thinking about solutions that don't involve any money at all. It turns out that fertilizer contains a lot of nitrogen and nearly all of Connecticut's field run-off drains into the Long Island Sound. The excess nitrogen results in algae blooms, which suck up the oxygen and kill the fish. So clearly our farmers must be to blame, right? Wrong.

A short visit from the Farm Bureau enlightened us to the use of fertilizer. It is expensive, so farmers are trained in its use so they don't overuse it. As a result, run-off just doesn't happen very often. So who is the culprit here? To paraphrase one of my favorite characters from the comic strip "Pogo," "we have met the enemy and he is us." More precisely, the enemy is every homeowner dying for that perfect green lawn. In pursuit of that goal, many gardeners tend to think more is better in terms of fertilizer. Why use just one bag when you can use two? Forget about what's actually recommended on the bag itself!

So what is a low-cost way to raise awareness? Stores that carry fertilizer can post signs alerting homeowners to the consequences of overuse. But why stop there? Why not get the kids involved. We all know how kids love to tell their parents what they are doing wrong. Engaging kids in a poster contest at school on the evils of too much fertilizer turned out to be a winner. This even prompted discussions about the importance of storm drains in preventing refuse from entering the Long Island Sound. What started out as kids play is now an annual occurrence.

Did we end up investing more in our stationary plants? Yup. But only after a thorough RBA review. However, our low-cost/no-cost solution really raised the level of enthusiasm and made everyone put their thinking cap on! And it worked.

Why This Is the Perfect Time to Think in Terms of Results (or It's the Economy, Stupid)

I taught economics for over twenty years. It's known as the "dismal science" that either fascinates people, or scares the living daylights out of them. It's the lens through which I view a lot of legislative decisions. When I need to defend a new effective program with up-front costs but long-term benefits, it's a blessing. When I have to sit through another dumb presentation for a program that I *know* has no added value, it's a curse.

The most valuable lesson I've learned from teaching economics is the ability to put it in terms everybody could understand. We should be able to explain our decisions just as easily to "no-degrees" as we can to Ph.D.'s.

I would always tell my economics students that I didn't want them to come away from my class having memorized a ridiculous number of formulas. I wanted them to be able to *think* like an economist. And I don't mean think like a brainiac, pie-in-the-sky academic, but a careful, analytic decision-maker. This skill has often served me well for legislative debate, as well as for getting my colleagues to think in terms of results.

I carried this message forward to the legislature by espousing the RBA methodology, which was accessible to all, and hammering home the "think in terms of results" message.

When you make legislative decisions in terms of results, what you're really doing is making economic decisions. To paraphrase James Carville, President Clinton's top political adviser, "it's the economy, stupid!"

Anyone reading newspaper headlines can figure this out.

Front Page: "Global Economic Crisis!"

Local News Page: "State government in debt!"

Education Page: "Cost of College Degree Plunging Graduates into Insurmountable Debt!"

Housing Page: "Economy Slow to Recover from Sub-Prime Mortgages!"

And so on...

You get the picture. I could bore you with a long-winded discussion of the effects of collateralized debt obligations, sovereign debt crises, and bailout packages, until your eyes crossed. But you don't need to know all that. All you need to know is that tackling these problems requires us to first identify the results we want and then work our way backwards to determine the means to achieve them.

In the midst of all this, what can government actually do? Political debate about government response always seems to be about choosing sides. More debt or less debt. Higher interest rates or lower interest rates. More taxes or less taxes. Instead of talking about what actually drives our economy, we end up in a meaningless debate about the size of government.

So ignore what the pundits and ideologues have to say. It's all BS. Remember, your job is to think like an economist!

And what do economists think about? They focus on what stimulates our economy: aggregate demand. It's the value of all the goods and services that you and I want and are willing to pay for. Let's break "aggregate demand" down into three parts.

First, there is consumption, the total amount that consumers spend on all goods and services. This includes all the purchases that your household makes. Some of them are often a tad ridiculous like a marshmallow air gun for the kids, and some of them are necessities like clothes, food, or housing.

The second part is investment. Investment, in this sense, doesn't mean stocks and bonds, but rather business spending on capital items such as new buildings or computer systems. Businesses "invest" in these resources to expand their capacity to sell you more stuff.

The third part is government spending, which runs the gamut from buying pencils for federal staffers to footing the bill for the war in Afghanistan.

All of these components are related. When consumers buy more goods and services, business can afford to invest in the infrastructure or equipment that will help them grow. When businesses grow, the government earns more in taxes that they can use to pay for new roads, schools, military supplies, etc. If one of these components is lagging, the others can hopefully pick up the slack.

But what happens when people, for whatever reason, lose confidence in the economy? If consumers don't feel secure in their jobs or economic outlook, spending slows. When their spending slows, business suffers. And I don't mean just the big, faceless, corporate conglomerates. I mean the local butchers, bakers, and candlestick makers. This is what economists mean when they say the economy is "consumption driven." Household spending drives growth. So when consumer confidence goes down the toilet, the economy is sure to follow.

So once that confidence takes a dive, the news alerts everyone to the downturn. And then consumer confidence dips even further. What was initially uncertainty in the economy is now distrust. It's a classic chicken and egg situation. Who is going to be the first to run out and buy a house when the housing market is on a downturn? Who is going to splurge and go on a lavish vacation when the economy appears to be tanking? Getting consumer confidence back is a really tough nut to crack.

I know what you're thinking. Well, if consumer confidence is in trouble, can investment come to the rescue? Let's look at this from the reverse. When the economy is racing along and the future looks rosy, of course the average business would look favorably on a new warehouse, new systems, and other capital investments.

However, all of those decisions rest on the assumption that people will continue buying goods and services. Remember, the bottom line for every business is maximizing profits, not spending money on facilities. If the CEO of Apple could meet the consumer demand for all the iPads by producing them in the trunk of his car, he wouldn't bother with a factory, would he? He only does so, when the investment allows him to make more profit.

That's why investment can be a double-edged sword. It's incredibly sensitive to demand trends. If demand rises, investment allows you to expand your capacity to sell. That means more money. But if demand falls, well, you're sore out of luck. I bet you're starting to see the problem here. If you have a situation like the sub-prime mortgage debacle, which feeds into a lack of consumer confidence, that insecurity can be infectious and businesses are not immune! Businesses will be more inclined to eat up inventory in order to weather the storm, rather than expand investments in capital. Even the Federal Reserve can try to keep interest rates exceedingly low and you still won't see investment happening if there is not a healthy dose of that confidence.

So if investment doesn't help, how does government spending fit into the picture? Government spending can be used to create confidence in the economy but with one big caveat. The spending has to be on programs that invest in the future, not the kind of "bridge-to-nowhere" or pork-barrel spending with some politician's name on it. It involves spending on things like infrastructure, multi-modal transportation, reducing student debt upon graduation, and earned income tax credits for the working poor. These are programs that stimulate the economy, get results, and restore faith in the country and the economy. And that is where it is critical that states focus on results informed decision- making.

Adding a program that doesn't work is one more nail in the coffin of consumer and business confidence. When we say we are going to create jobs, we should actually see unemployment rates go down. When we say we are going to reduce out of state placement for our most vulnerable kids, we actually have to see our own school rolls grow. When we say abuse and neglect is a problem we have to be able to show through data that at the end of the day we can make families better off.

The question isn't whether government spending is good or bad, but whether government spending gets results. After all, how can you manage what you can't (or refuse) to measure? The Connecticut legislature's Committee on Children has been working on a data-informed "Children's RBA Report Card." That alone may not sound impressive, but the fact that it has the full support of our Department of Children and Families is a damn-near Christmas miracle. The legislature and the agency have an interest in knowing what is working and what isn't.

The Children's RBA Report Card unearthed some surprising trends. As we were looking at, the *Results Statement*, "A Stable Living Environment," chronic absenteeism (defined as being absent at least 9 days a semester) came up as a possible indicator, so we looked up the statistic. We couldn't have imagined that on average 15% of students were chronically absent in Connecticut, missing a minimum of 10% of the school-year. We found rates as high as 25% for African American students and 26% for Latino students, and a whopping 27% for kids on free and reduced lunch. But placing the blame on the Department of Education would pretty much guarantee they would never work with us again. We could see this pitfall from a mile away and weren't going to fall in. Instead, we met with the commissioner and discussed a pilot program and different ways to move forward. We knew there were programs getting good results so we decided to focus on expanding those by working in consultation with the department.

Another success was working with the Department of Children and Families (DCF). By coming together to "turn the curve" on issues like out-of-state placement of children and promotion of foster and kinship care, we achieved results that folks had been working toward for nearly twenty years by getting kids back with their families and saving money for the state. I had legislators turn to me in my role as co-Chair of the Committee on Children and ask, "What magic button did you push?" And believe me, when you start showing results like that, people start caring more about the *effect* and less about the *expenditure*.

The lesson here is that all the talk about good government spending, bad government spending or even mediocre government spending misses the point. In a faltering economy, the only kind of government spending that matters is the type that gets *results*—real, tangible, meaningful results.

Sorry, if I burst your bubble, but there are no shortcuts. You can't just throw money at the problem and walk away. We desperately want to hang onto the old way of doing things, but that's how we've ended up with bloated "grow-as- you-go" incremental budgets. It's familiar, it's comfortable, and it doesn't threaten the status quo. But more importantly, it doesn't work. This type of business-as-usual mindset lets you off the hook of identifying the programs that merit government funding and the ones that are simply dead weight.

So don't just gaze out of the windows of the bus while the budget continues to grow or gets randomly cut killing good programs along with the bad. Legislators and policy-makers actually have to choose a route for the government bus to take. Do the research. Get the numbers. Make the case. Then make sure that the programs you are funding are actually getting us to the end or destination that you have chosen.

The economy really does rest on confidence, and it is the job of government to protect and build that confidence when it starts to wear away. All of this is even more important in our shared and seamless world. Now more than ever, our economy operates globally. You push the balloon in China, and it pops out in California. Global forces bring a whole new level of complexity that requires an ability to manage our internal affairs, in light of everything else going on that may be beyond our control.

5

Build It and They
Will Come...Not

In the interest of full disclosure, we made a few mistakes along the road to RBA success. I know. Perish the thought that legislators would ever make any mistakes but, wonder of wonders, we did.

Denise Merrill, the former House Chair of the Appropriations Committe (and current Connecticut Secretary of State), and I returned from our "budget epiphany on the West Coast," at NCSL feeling a bit like Lavern and Shirley. This was not just a function of ridiculous cross-country traveling misadventures but also our now rather frenetic desire to implement, without delay, this very cool new RBA tool we had discovered.

We were on a mission, but both of us knew that there were obstacles ahead—not the least of which would be legislators' renowned limited attention span. Now, I could attribute that wandering state of consciousness to legislators, being underpaid and overworked or needing to be mini experts in a zillion areas which requires us to jump from subject to subject with frightening speed. This is all true, but there is something else at play here.

Legislators tend to behave much like six year olds being introduced to the finer points of soccer. At first, they nod with owl-like concentration. When the game begins , however, any instruction given on field position gets thrown out the window, and they all go out and chase the ball—the ball in this case being a legislator's latest pet project.

We knew we had to come up with a format that would capture legislator's attention in as simple and direct way as possible, otherwise they would never see their way to the merits of actually implementing an accountability model. Remember, it is much easier to talk about the importance of accountability rather than actually being accountable. It should come as no surprise that most legislators have perfected "all talk and no action" as an essential part of their skill set.

Mark Friedman, the RBA guru, does fabulous training sessions on accountability. He actually makes the whole system seem like fun even though the presentation is full of information. He leads you through a discussion of accountability by connecting the simple example of fixing a leaky roof to the very robust example of solving Gordian knots of public policy. He takes you from talk to action in terms that even your most recalcitrant legislator or staffer cannot deny understanding.

So, Denise and I thought this was truly simple. Bring Mark to Connecticut and watch the sparks fly. How cool would that be? We could sit in the audience and congratulate ourselves (which we did) and reap praise on how awesome this new accountability system appeared.

We brought Mark back several times to be sure that legislators and staff had ample opportunity to be trained in this wondrous tool we had found. We enlisted a consultant, the Charter Oak Group who was willing to take the accountability plunge with us. We didn't get all legislators and staff trained, but we felt we had engaged enough of them to take it to the next level - our first full meeting of the Appropriations Committee.

Well, for starters we have joint committees in Connecticut, so there is a Senate Chair of Appropriations, Senator Harp, who would need to be involved as well. In our endless enthusiasm, Denise and I forgot that. Senator Harp's first peek at RBA gave her the impression that it would be used as a tool to cut programs, particularly the social programs dear to her heart. She was known to be smart and reasonable so before she got really upset we went and spoke with her.

We assumed that RBA was so obviously incredible that we really didn't need to do any lobbying or in-depth explanations of what it does with our peers in leadership. We assumed that absolutely everyone just couldn't wait to jump on the accountability bus with us. No need for laborious explanations—accountability speaks for itself!

In retrospect, it seems like such an elementary thing to almost get tripped up on, but we did. Not having the Senate chair totally on board would have been a disaster.

Fortunately, we took the time to sit down and speak with Senator Harp. We explained that the primary focus of RBA is on finding programs that work so that you could repurpose money away from programs that don't work. As a result of our conversation we painted a whole new picture of RBA for her.

When we pointed out that this was not an exercise in seeing how much you could cut, but in finding out how we make the people of Connecticut better off in a measurable way, she was on board. She is now a RBA champion who has done amazing work on furthering the use of this accountability tool.

So, don't ever forget to incude leadership. Take the time for full explanations and in-depth looks at how the process works!

Having gotten over that hurdle, we were on our way to the first meeting thoroughly prepared with all our knowledge of getting from talk to action in the most simple direct way possible. Guess what? We proceeded to do just the opposite.

I can clearly remember our Appropriations Committee maven, Susan Keane, on the morning of the full appropriations meeting giving me this "you-have-to- be kidding" look as I arrived to prep for the meeting. I didn't understand until I saw books of information being collated for the meeting. This certainly didn't look like getting from talk to action. But it sure did look like our normal information overload, which inevitably ended up on legislators' shelves collecting dust.

What happened?

The old mental software had kicked in and, apparently, no matter how many times we had been to the trainings we couldn't help from spitting out reams of excess information.

How could we be there on the morning of the meeting with papers flying around, borrowing clerks and legislative assistants from every corner of the building to help organize these huge notebooks of information? We knew better. A couple of times that morning, I actually thought I saw Susan's eyes directing laser death rays at our consultant, who was trying his damnedest to look like everything was under control.

We supposedly knew better, but we were all neophytes in the great arena of accountability and felt that regardless of all that training there was a slew of information that we absolutely had to provide or the Appropriations Committee would never understand the value of RBA.

I can still remember the bemused expressions on the faces of Appropriations Committee members as they leafed through these tomes and periodically looked up to try to capture some of the information being presented. Not a good sign!

We had engaged the guru of accountability for our training sessions, so we knew where we needed to go, yet we let the system take over. These are the inevitable growing pains of changing a system. At the time we were too close to the process to recognize it and were left wondering how everything was going in the wrong direction and how the hell we could get back on track.

It is all about discipline. If there is one way to express an idea, find it, and ignore the twenty-two ways you thought you needed. When I am told that a system has seventy-five indicators for one outcome my first thought is "been there, done that, and it ain't gonna work." Our first foray into accountability, even though it was a bit of a disaster, was a great training tool in how *not* to do it. Yes, we had to find our way out of the rabbit hole we had created but we learned a lot on our way out.

Never underestimate how data presented concisely and concretely can lure legislators into paying attention. Brevity is its own reward. I know, it is tough to strip out what you think is essential information, but remember that information is always still available to the interested legislator or staffer. What you need to do is find the most compelling data-rich indicators and present them in a comprehensive and digestible fashion.

We encountered more false starts as we tried to build a template that our agencies could work with and that was concise enough for legislators to quickly grasp. The agencies were still wondering what the hell was going on and whether we were really trying to change things. Regardless of the trainings, they retreated to what they knew best, trying to lay low until we'd move on to something else, aka the "WeBe" trap.

Initially, we kept coming up with lengthy templates that obscured more than they revealed. We could not understand why our brilliance was not being rewarded with stunning insights into the inner workings of state programs.

I assure you, the more complex the template, the more opportunities stubborn agencies will have to sneak back down the rabbit hole and legislators will have to nod off into their sixth cup of coffee.

For instance, I had one legislator ask me if I could explain "just one more time" how I knew what the red arrow next to an indicator meant and what the green arrow next to another indicator meant. At first I thought it was a joke and that I was on candid camera until I realized it was a real question. Wow. If that didn't show the template wasn't working, I don't know what would.

So we simplified and we tapped as many minds as we could, because fresh eyes can sometimes make a world of difference. Our Program Review and Investigations Committee staff were the first ones to crack the nut. I had reached out to them to do a study on some Department of Children & Families programs (I sit on the Oversight Committee, which always helps) and asked them to submit it in a RBA format. I knew that their analysts would be looking for the best possible way to organize the material and that they had our evolving prototype in hand. Well they were brilliant, particularly Jill Jensen, a senior analyst, who is now part of the Children's Report Card leadership team (You will meet her again in the next chapter). They got it right, and with the essential help of our OFA analysts, we were able to refine their contribution just a bit more. We now have a template that I think you will find invaluable (Last part of Appendix C).

Regardless of whether agencies are being deliberately obtuse or honestly confused, if you don't have a straight forward template, you will lose the battle before it begins, giving agencies ample reason to whine to the executive and put off the legislature.

6

The Connecticut Children's Report Card

I f you've hung in there and actually read the book this far, here is the reward: the story of how we got the Connecticut Children's Report Card, the signature accomplishment of the Connecticut General Assembly's Committee on Children. In case you don't remember, I am the House Chair of said committee.

Recall that we resisted putting RBA in statute. The perception that legislators love to mandate something and then never check to see what has actually transpired is largely true. So we worked on RBA in the Appropriations Committee without resorting to putting it into statute until we felt that colleagues and bureaucrats got the message. We simply were not going to drop this disruptive idea that government should be accountable. This was after many sessions spent embedding RBA in forty-seven state agencies!

I have a particular perception derived from my years as a college professor teaching economics and environmental issues. Virtually all of my classes gave the same answer when asked how to get people to care what happens to our world while balancing economic development and a healthy environment. The response: teach your children well (yup, I am a Crosby, Stills, Nash and Young fan).

Seriously, when my students examined all of the fancy economic models and environmental disasters and then framed them within a legislative process that our forefathers meant to be slow and deliberate (and Washington, D.C., has managed to take to new heights) they have always agreed: unless we start early with this information, we will continue to simply muddle through and the result will be legislatures that career from crisis to crisis.

This is coupled with the statement heard *ad naseum* during campaigns that "our children are our future." This one really gets to me when I watch programs for kids jettisoned in a heartbeat...remember the battle over the S-CHIP program?

I had a wonderful experience with a group of fourth graders discussing children's issues. I used the phrase, "People need to 'man up' when it comes to kid's issues," meaning we actually have to follow through and vote the way we talk.

One young girl patiently waited her turn to speak to me. As she stepped up, it was clear from her very unusual outfit that she was a budding free spirit. As I marveled at her striped socks and multi colored skirt she piped up, "Representative Urban, what we really need is for people to 'woman up.' Many times I have wished that I could have her on tap to bring this classic women's message to recalcitrant committees!

When will we realize that kids actually get it?

If you really do believe that children are our future and you really do care about making sure that there is some kind of intergenerational equity, what can you do to focus attention and policy on our kids? Simple. Build a RBA based report card that creates a structure for where you want your state to go and then see if your programs are actually getting you there.

As it turned out, we had another reason to go there ourselves. When we asked the Legislative Program Review and Investigations Committee (PRI) to do the Department of Children & Families (DCF) studies, it came up with an amazing budget number for a small state. We were spending $5.8 billion annually on child and family welfare programs, but we had no idea how well those programs were working. We figured if the $5.8 billion number couldn't capture legislators' attention, nothing could.

We therefore decided it was time to put our RBA Children's Report Card efforts into bill form and try to get it through the committee process and on to the floor of the House and the Senate.

Well, our first try fell short; we got the bill out of the House, but the Senate did not take it up. Senator Bob Duff, my Appropriations RBA subcommittee co-Chair, and I realized that getting it into law was going to be a heavier lift than we first envisioned. Remember, however, that my co-chair was also my secret weapon, "The Enforcer."

The next session we again put the bill forward, but this time as a Children's Committee bill. While the initial bill had come out of the PRI Committee, we thought that starting it in the Committee on Children not only would give it more gravitas but also gave me control of the bill as it wound it's way through the process. I cannot emphasize enough the importance of this decision. As the session gathers speed it is essential to have a way to highlight your bill and as chair of the Committee on Children, I knew that introducing it through our committee, would put the focus smack dab on kids. We should have thought of this the first time around, but my legislative learning curve is always evolving!

As is usually the case, committee chairs are tracking numerous bills. We had just gotten Joette Katz, as our extraordinary new DCF Commissioner and she was bent on reorganizing the agency. Our DCF had a pretty dismal history including being under court order (the 'Juan F' case). Since my Committee on Children co-Chair, Senator Gerratana, and I supported giving Joette that ability her efforts definitely took priority on my "to do bill list," and we focused on getting the agency bills out.

In the midst of this, I brought the Children's Report Card bill out in the House and it sailed through unanimously. So far, so good. Then we ran headlong into the notorious end-of-session legislative crawl, where the minority party slows things down procedurally so the majority has to deal with them or listen to seven hour "debates" about minutia. This means a short life for important bills, unless you are willing to make many trips between the House and the Senate to keep your bills on track in a growing legislative queue. This also meant I couldn't work the Children's Report Card bill in the Senate because I was way too busy shepherding the DCF bills.

When pushing policy, it is so important to work with the right people. As the session drew to a close, I was running down the hall of the Senate trying to track down some key votes when my RBA subcommittee co-Chair Senator Duff passed me and called out, "You know that Children's Report Card bill? Well, I got it on the Senate consent calendar."

For those of you unfamiliar with our legislative process, the consent calendar is GOLD as it means the bill has been agreed upon by both caucuses and is basically law. To say I was stunned is putting it mildly.

And then he smiled, and asked, "Are you okay with that?" Holy Moly, talk about delivering! I will never be able to give him enough credit; he was absolutely masterful. The only credit that I can take is that I was the one who reached out to him in the beginning to join me (as my "Enforcer") on the RBA journey. Yet again it is a team effort, and the team you build is so important!

We now had in statute PA11-109 "An Act Requiring an Annual RBA Report Card Evaluating State Policies and Programs Impacting Children" signed, sealed and delivered with the governor's signature. I had given my committee the responsibility to actually deliver this Children's Report Card, so the fun began in earnest.

We formed a working group and made sure it was totally inclusive. The first meeting was amazing because all of the stakeholders were taking it seriously. Seventy-five people showed up and stayed until we finished. I believe a big reason for their continued attendance was my unwavering commitment to keeping the meetings to an hour and fifteen minutes, without exception.

After six months of meetings, we collectively agreed upon our *Population Results* statement for Connecticut, "All Connecticut Children Grow Up In Stable Environments, Safe, Healthy And Ready to Succeed." One of the things I love about RBA is that because you start at a point of agreement, the process begins on a collaborative note, and not a confrontational one. Those four results from the statement became our four domains (Stable, Safe, Healthy, Ready to Succeed) and we built baselines and indicators to show how close (or far away) we were to actually reaching the *Population Result*.

Yet again, my luck held up as four amazing people stepped up to become our leadership team. They were: Erika Bromley, Youth Services Director from Middletown, Dr. Christine Dauser from Yale University, Anne McIntyre-Lahner a director from the Department of Children and Families and Brian Hill the Deputy Director of our Court Support Services Division. We then added a person you met in the last chapter, Jill Jensen, a PRI Senior Policy Analyst because I desperately needed someone familiar with RBA to oversee the final touches. Jill had just retired and one of our partners, David Nee at the Graustein Memorial Fund, offered to help get her back part-time. I am not sure this is exactly what Jill had in mind when she retired, but I was thrilled to tap into her enormous skill set. Finally, I rounded off the team with Liz Giannaros our wonderful Committee on Children clerk who used her incredible organizational skills and soft touch to nudge me along when the going got rough.

To top it all off, I got a sessional committee clerk, Breana Vessichio, on her way to law school who was totally into rocking the boat of conventional policy with us. She was another gift, and I'd keep her if I could but in the interest of all women policy makers, the girl had to go on to law school. While we had her, she was an amazing addition. As luck would have it we then somehow managed to get an intern assigned to the committee, Alessandra Burgett . She was working on completion of her MSW and turned out to be an energetic data geek extraordinaire! So meet our new Special Projects Assistant! The message? Remember to engage the young people. It is worth it!

In yet another stroke of luck, when my venerable Senate chair, Terry Gerratana moved on, I got an amazing freshman senator, Dante Bartolomeo, as my new co-Chair. She has an impressive background in kids' issues which perfectly compliments my penchant for data-driven analysis. We immediately became a potent team. I am starting to believe it might not just be luck. It could be that new age stuff about positive energy begetting positive energy!

I simply don't know what I would have done without these smart, dedicated worker bees, staffers, legislative colleagues, and a generous, committed foundation!

Although Connecticut was ranked seventh in the nation on the Annie E. Casey Foundation Kids Count survey when we began our analysis, it became clear that we had major problems, particularly when it came to minorities and children living in poverty. The achievement gap is a revealing measure of the difference in school achievement between minority students and their Caucasian peers. The disturbing statistic in which we, one of the wealthiest states in the country, had the worst achievement gap cast a whole new light on the need to solve this problem.

As we built out the indicators we found some incredibly instructive things. For example, as mentioned earlier, we learned that we were not adequately addressing chronic absenteeism. A little more digging showed that the number one problem causing kids to miss school was asthma. Another RBA study revealed that school based health centers were the answer to keeping these kids in school and avoiding the future problems that being chronically absent causes. We also found we were placing too much emphasis on child abuse and not enough on child neglect, which is often the first indicator of future abuse.

As for the result, I won't spoil it for you, you can see for yourself at the website http://www.ctkidsreportcard.org. The *Population Structure* is almost complete, and we have begun the process of looking at the performance of programs that contribute to the *Population Result*. This is where the template I mentioned comes into play.

Agencies and providers alike are asked the three fundamental questions: How much did you do? How well did you do it? Is anyone better off? Eventually every children's program in the state that accepts state money will have to report its results to our Children's Report Card using a template that limits each program to two pages. As you might guess, this is a legislator's dream come true.

And by the way, we are the only legislature in the country to take children's issues to the next level and create a results-driven Children's Report Card. How cool is that?

In addition, I can't emphasize enough how important it is to keep upping your visibility when dealing with the General Assembly. Remember that penchant for wandering attention spans! We formed a high level Children's Report Card Strategic Leadership Group and managed to get our dynamic, venerable, universally respected Lt. Governor Nancy Wyman to co-chair it with our equally well-versed children's advocate David Nee. Talk about gravitas... we were filled to the brim!

In an outgrowth of the Children's Report Card, my new co-Chair and I upped the stakes in our committee.

If we were truly going to pursue data informed decision-making we needed to be sure that testimony in front of our committee was actually based in fact. And that the studies quoted or referred to were legitimate. So we introduced "Questions for the Record," loosely based on a similar federal tool.

In Connecticut, public hearings testimony is followed by legislative questions. When the committee members have asked all their questions, if any are based on data or studies presented in the testimony we inform the presenter that we are asking a "Question for the Record," which requires an answer. We direct our clerk to make note of that and to follow up. We actually have an Excel spreadsheet available to everyone to keep track of the questions and responses.

Our new tool led to the rumor in the capitol that the Committee on Children was making people do homework. As long as we are focused on transparency and accountability and doing the best job we can for the children and families in Connecticut, "Questions for the Record" is here to stay!

Conclusion

I began this book with a rhetorical question: who's driving the bus? And if I belabored the theme over the preceding pages, well, I meant to. For all its inelegance, the question encapsulates the attributes—including leadership, purpose and trustworthiness—to which our elected officials should aspire and that we should demand (if not always, at least most of the time). Just as bus drivers are expected to, at a minimum, deliver us to our destinations safely, it seems reasonable that we should expect as much from our elected representatives.

Executives, legislatures, and agencies across all levels of government should know what ends and outcomes they want to achieve to improve the lives of their constituents.

Put another way, they should know their "destination." They should use consistent means and follow optimal routes if they are to have any chance of meeting those outcomes. And that means we expect them to know what roads they plan on taking.

At all times they should honor that well-worn provision from the Hippocratic Oath, "First, do no harm," or as we would say, they should try not to crash or hurt any passengers along the way.

The frustrating truth, of course, is that government too often fails to satisfy even these basic expectations. The executive and legislative branches aren't on the same page. Agencies and political parties have their own agendas and turf battles (there are egos and naked ambition everywhere). And of course spending is ineffective. Bad programs persist even when there is evidence they don't work; good programs languish even when there is evidence that they do work. So when posed in reference to government, my titular question is often leveled as an accusation. As in, the bus may be moving but there's no one behind the wheel, and you're wasting my money!

Why is this the case? Well, elected officials aren't intentionally putting driverless buses on the road to idle, meander or crash, while wasting public resources. Sure, most of us are inveterate pains-in-the-ass and there are clearly real divisions between Democrats and Republicans that will occasionally produce gridlock. But if demand for Connecticut's results-based story is any indication, I'd say that legislators across all levels of government and both sides of the aisle are generally well intentioned and want to figure out how to make things work better (or at least to expend public resources much more effectively).

The problem is that conflict between branches, parties and agencies, as well as institutionalized behaviors throughout the system, stack the odds against transformational change. And adoption of ends-to-means thinking and result-based accountability approaches require a paradigm shift that can feel like trying to turn a cruise ship with a canoe paddle. Put crudely, the crush of legislative business, fundraising, and, of course, general politicking mean that most elected officials have neither the time nor the stomach to fight against that current. In the end, it's a lot easier to muddle through with the status quo than to build the expertise and support necessary to fundamentally change the way that the state (or county or city) business gets done.

Given these rather durable barriers, you're probably asking yourself: why bother? Truth be told, if I hadn't been front and center during Connecticut's adoption of results-based thinking, I'd probably be skeptical too. But the Connecticut case provides evidence that governments can harness their budgeting and appropriations processes to focus on results. In other words, it is possible to implement and institutionalize ends-to-means thinking and results-based budgeting in ways that increase the efficiency and effectiveness of the public sector. Doing so is certainly hard and takes time. False starts and resets are inevitable. And even once you've got the thing up and running, maintenance can be a bear. But it can happen. And the benefits, in terms of both well-functioning government and improved conditions for citizens, are well worth the effort.

Although I've taken pains not to write a step-by-step "how-to" guide, there are lessons to be distilled from my experience, particularly for those of you just getting started. Chief among them are the following:

- Learn all you can about the Results Based Accountability approach (see www.raguide.org and read "Trying Hard Is Not Good Enough" by Mark Friedman)

- Find an RBA guru (I'm biased toward a legislature-led process, but if your executive wants to take the lead, by all means, partner with him or her)

- Engage allies (and whenever necessary, sweet-talk opponents)

- Start small (don't overpromise, don't overreach and, if possible, start with a pilot project; take to scale when you know you're ready).

- Be clear and consistent (agree on a common language and use it; make the rules of the game transparent; apply the rules equitably).

■ Be realistic (select results, indicators and performance measures that you and your constituents understand and think are important, and that you have a reasonable chance of moving in relatively short order).

■ Be humble (acknowledge that this is hard work; publicly support efforts to engage in the process; resist grand-standing).

■ Stay committed (don't let set-backs, resistance, or even election cycles derail your efforts).

And while I can't promise that following these lessons will produce the same results we've seen, I can at least guarantee that they'll give you a fighting chance!

In closing, let me say once again how proud I am that the Connecticut legislature led our state's effort to adopt a results-based model and even prouder that we have sustained it through numerous election cycles, including turn-over in the governor's mansion. Over the last several years, we have employed ends-to-means decision-making to achieve, you guessed it, results that are and will continue to benefit our citizens. We have kept the legislature and agencies committed to the process and are getting to ends and outcomes - and turning off a whole fleet of idling buses - much more efficiently than ever before. And while I can't say I love the ongoing maintenance, it does keep RBA a priority in our budgeting and performance management efforts and will remain an indispensible element of our experience and success.

SUPPORTING CONNECTICUT KIDS AND FAMILIES

RBA

Epilogue

As the Connecticut Kids Report Card makes its way into the mainstream, I get many requests to address leadership classes, clinics, forums and so forth on the basic, "Wow, can you tell us how you did this?" People are particularly impressed (if not stunned) that the effort was, and is, being lead by the legislature.

This kind of initiative is almost always lead by the chief executive because he or she can tell his or her agencies, "just do it," which effectively ends the discussion. Assuming he or she has a crack data team, it's "game over."

For a legislature, however, that is just the beginning. In Connecticut we started in the Appropriations Committee which was an excellent decision - money always makes everyone a tad more attentive .In addition, we adhered to Churchill's famous advice: "Never give in–never, never, never, never, in nothing great or small, large or petty, never give in except to convictions of honour and good sense."

Along with money and that level of tenacity, there was another variable at work. I guess it was a combination of my personality and the willingness of a few organizations to actually listen to me.

As you may recall, I was trying to figure out how the hell I could reintroduce a performance system that was already in our Connecticut statute. I ultimately decided just to keep tweaking the original language using the infamous "amendment path to success." It was about that time ,as I was starting to think this was never going to work, that I saw an advertisement in *Governing Magazine* for their annual Government Performance Summit in Texas.

Perfect! I thought, "I will call them and ask if I can present on how hard it is to get performance work done. It will give me the opportunity to pick some other minds." Remember, I was a freshman legislator - it seemed incredibly reasonable to me that making this "ask" would work.

I will never forget the phone call I made to Elder Witt, who was editor at the time. She said it was great that I had reached out to *Governing Magazine*, but that they usually liked to have people present on issues at their summits who had experienced some success. I didn't have much of a rejoinder to that except to say that I was trying really hard.

To her credit, she said she would get back to me. "Sure," I thought, "That will be when pigs fly."

About a week later she called back! She said that she had discussed it with the "powers that be" and that they thought if I had the guts to ask, they had the guts to respond. The next thing I knew, I was going to Texas.

Thus began an association that has been critical for me. *Governing Magazine's* imprimatur provided me with some cachet but more importantly with access to a phalanx of experts in all aspects of government from all over the country. Jonathan Walters, Richard Greene, and Katherine Barrett top the list.

The lesson here is that we need more of that kind of support. NCSL does some great work, as do CSG and many other organizations, but I would love to have an umbrella organization to coordinate efforts. I was a Flemmings Fellow, and it was a super experience. But securing funding to sustain organizations like it is always a problem. An umbrella organization helping to manage fundraising would alleviate the fragmentation that occurs now as individual groups compete for limited dollars.

By that I mean make the critical follow-up call or meeting after the "informational summit" to encourage the legislators tenacious enough to keep trying. Issue papers are wonderful and information on what other states are doing is useful, but we could do better.

Legislators need this support because we are enormously pressed for time. We usually have only a few months to do what the executive branch spends all year working on. So come to us! We don't always have the time for a gathering in Chicago or Atlanta, and even if it occurs when we are out of session, we also need the support when we are in session! How about Skype? Use technology creatively and find people who have "been there and done that" to help these committed, energetic legislators to succeed.

Finally, no academics! I should know - I am one.

Bringing in a Ph.D. just annoys legislators. Remember, legislators come from every walk of life and their most common characteristic is a healthy dose of common sense. You need some of the people who have been in Teddy Roosevelt's "arena." These are the folks who have been beaten up by the system and are crazy enough to figure out how to keep moving the ball forward, while willing to help nurture other brave souls.

In other words, find and support the people who, for whatever reason, are the true public servants. Service is in their heart; it is a core value.

If we do this, I think we could change the world!

Appendix A

Four Questions Every State Legislature Should Be Asking to get Results

1. How is our state doing on each respective result?

   ■ For each indicator, what is the historic baseline and what is your forecast (factoring in trends and any anticipated changes but otherwise assuming no significant additional changes in our current level of effort in our state).

   ■ What other data (i.e., indicators) might we need in order to measure progress toward this result?

2. What is the story behind the historic baselines and forecasts for the indicators?

- Given what we know or can surmise about the result, what are the causes and forces at work (contributing and restraining) that explain our state's current situation?

- We are especially interested in your identification of the most significant "root causes" and in your prioritization of those causes in order of significance.

3. What will it take to improve the current situation on the respective result?

- What has worked elsewhere?

- What do you think would work in our state (including actions of governmental and non-governmental partners and no cost and low cost actions)?

- What could the legislature do?

- What would be the most important elements of an integrated, multi-year strategy across agencies and in collaboration with national, state, and local partners in the public and private sectors?

4. What do you propose to do to "turn the curve" of the indicators?

- What is your integrated, multi-year strategy?

- How will your strategy address the most significant root causes you identified in your analysis?

▌ What will you be doing that is different?

▌ How will you collaborate with your peers and community partners?

▌ What is your timeline, deliverables and performance measures for the key elements of the strategy?

▌ How much will it cost?

Appendix B

*Glossary of RBA Terms Used in Connecticut**

Connecticut Appropriations Committee

The Language of Accountability

The most common problem in Results-Based Accountability or any similar work is the problem of language. People come to the table from many different disciplines and many different walks of life. And the way in which we talk about pro-

*Adopted from Mark Friedman's Results Accountability Implementation Guide, http://www.raguide.org/RA/the_language_of_accountability.htm Rev. 1 (12/31/11) Page 2

grams, services and populations varies all over the map. This means that the usual state of affairs in planning for children, families, adults, elders and communities is a Tower of Babel, where no one really knows what the other person is saying, but everyone politely pretends that they do. As a consequence, the work is slow, frustrating, and often ineffective.

It is possible to exercise language discipline. And the way to do this is to *agree on a set of definitions that start with ideas and not words.* Words are just labels for ideas. And the same idea can have many different labels. The following nine ideas are central to RBA. The labels for these ideas are those chosen by the Appropriations Committee in Connecticut to ensure that everyone means the same thing when they use these ideas. They are the same terms that Mark Friedman uses in all of his material.

Results *are conditions of well-being for entire populations — children, adults, families or communities —* stated in plain English, or any other language. They are things that voters and taxpayers can understand. They are not about programs or agencies or government jargon. Results include: healthy children, children ready for school, children succeeding in school, children staying out of trouble, strong families, elders living with dignity in settings they prefer, safe communities, a healthy, clean environment, a prosperous economy. *In Connecticut, we refer to population results or quality of life results.*

Indicators *are measures that help quantify the achievement of a population result.* They answer the question "How would we recognize these results in measurable terms if we fell over them?" So, for example, the rate of low-birth weight babies helps quantify whether we're getting healthy births. Third grade reading scores help quantify whether children are succeeding in school today and whether they were ready for school three years ago. The crime rate helps quantify whether we are living in safe communities. *Indicators refer only to whole populations, not programs.*

Strategies *are coherent collections of actions which have a reasoned chance of improving results.* Strategies are made up of *our best thinking about what works*, and they include the contributions of many partners. No single action by any one agency can create the improved results we want and need. Programs are not themselves strategies; they are expressions of strategies. *Programs are specific ways of implementing strategies*, usually targeted toward a specific sub-group within the population. For example, a strategy of family support may have as one expression the program Nurturing Families Network, which is targeted at new parents at risk of abusing or neglecting their newborn child.

Performance Measures *are measures of how well public and private programs and agencies are working.* The most important performance measures tell us whether the clients or customers of the program's service are better off. Measures that track the quality of the program are also important. *In Connecticut, we refer to measures of whether clients are better off as client or customer outcomes* (to distinguish them from population results for all children, adults or families). Performance measure can apply to individual programs, entire agencies, or service delivery systems.

Baselines *are what we call a trend line of an indicator or program measure when presented in a chart.* The baseline consists of the *history of the measure* (what the measure has been for the last 3-5 years) and the *forecast of where the measure will be* in 3-5 years if we keep doing what we are doing.

Story Behind the Baseline *is the diagnostic phase of RBA.* It identifies the causes and forces at work behind the current level of performance for an indicator. Without a clear understanding of what is causing the performance to be the way it is, any strategies or actions are likely to be just random good ideas.

Turning the Curve *describes efforts to improve the direction or rate of change in the baseline* of an indicator or performance measure. It is also shorthand for the process of determining whether the current and projected level on an indicator or performance measure is acceptable or requires change. We turn the curve with strategies and actions that are based on what works: what we know from the research, best practices, and our own experience is likely to address the story behind the baselines.

Ends and Means *are an important distinction in RBA.* Results and indicators are about the ends we want for children and families. Strategies, programs, and performance measures are about the means to get there. Processes that fail to make this crucial distinction often mix up ends and means. Ends are usually something everyone can agree on, e.g., people with better health, more education, safer streets. This agreement forms a common ground that allows the discussions to focus on the means, about which there are often legitimate differences of opinion that can be explored. Failed processes tend to get mired in a mixed discussion about ends and means that causes hopeless confusion and disillusionment. Clarity and discipline about language at the start will help you take your work *from talk to action.*

What about Mission and Vision, Values, Benchmarks, Goals, Objectives, Problems, Issues, Inputs and Outputs? Many of us have grown up with these traditional words in strategic planning and budgeting. Where do they fit? *Remember that words are just labels for ideas.* These ten words have no natural standard definitions that bridge across all the different ways they are used. They are terms of art which can and are used to label many different ideas. This is why we pay so much attention to getting language discipline straight at the very beginning. It's the ideas that are important, not the words. *To avoid confusion, Connecticut does not use these words in its RBA work.* For more information on how these words can be used in other contexts, see Mark Friedman's discussion of The Language of Accountability at http://www.raguide.org/RA/the_language_of_accountability.htm

Appendix C

2013 Program Report Card: Nurturing Families Network (Department of Social Services)

Quality of Life Result: All Connecticut children birth to age 9 grow up in a stable environment, safe, healthy, and ready to succeed.

Contribution to Result: The NFN provides intensive home visiting for high risk families to help solve problems, break the family's social isolation, prevent child abuse and neglect and ensure that children have a promising future.

Program Expenditures	State Funding	Federal Funding	Other Funding	Total Funding
Actual FY 12	10,383,000	600,000		10,983,000
Estimated FY 13	10,189,346	2,237,172		12,426,518

Partners: Nurturing Families Network infrastructure includes 40 sites operating within all 29 birthing hospitals and partners with dozens of public and private service centers.

How Much Did We Do?

Increase in number of families served each year and comparative number of families enrolling in home visiting services per year.

Figure 1. NFN Participation Rates (2007 – 2011)

2006 2007 2008 2009 2010 2011

— Families Starting HV services
— Families Served During the Year

Story behind the baseline: Along with an increase in the number of NFN sites, the number of families enrolling in home visiting services has increased from 563 in 2006 to 743 families in 2011. Additionally, the number of families served in home visiting has risen more than 69% from 2006 to 2011, with 1,201 participants in 2006 to 2,034 participants in 2011. There was a slight decrease in rates of participation in 2010 compared to 2009, which is likely related to the state budget uncertainty impacting sites, with an accompanying loss of staff (3 times more new staff were trained in 2010 compared to 2008) and consequently fewer participants.

Trend: ▲

Submitted Jan. 2013

How Well Did We Do It?

The program was successful in screening high-risk parents with rigid parenting attitudes

Figure 2. Parenting Rigidity: Mothers and Fathers (2007 – 2011)

2007 2008 2009 2010 2011

■ Mother's Parenting Rigidity
■ Father's Parenting Rigidity

Story behind the baseline: Scores on the Child Abuse Potential Rigidity (CAP-R) subscale indicate the level of rigid parenting attitudes, and consequently risk for maltreating children. The average score for a normative population on the CAP-R is 10.1 with a standard deviation of 12.5. The data in Figure 4 shows that NFN mothers (average score of 27) and fathers (average score of 32) come into the program with CAP-R scores more than twice the normative score (i.e. 10), indicating extremely high-risk populations. CAP -R outcomes are shown in figure 8 pm page 3.

Trend: ▲

Trend Going in Right Direction? ▲ Yes; ▼ No; ◄► Flat/ No Trend

How Well Did We Do It?

The program was successful in engaging parents with moderate to severe family stress.

Figure 3. Rate of Moderate to Severe Family Stress (2008 - 2011)

2008 2009 2010 2011

— Rate of Moderate to Severe Risk mothers
— Rate of Moderate to Severe Risk fathers

Story behind the baseline: Rates of moderate to severe family stress as measured by the Kempe Family Stress checklist are presented in Figure 5. These data show that over 60% of mothers score between the moderate to severe range in areas of multiple sources of stress including childhood history of abuse and neglect, social isolation, depression, and history of crime and substance abuse. While fathers report lower rates of moderate to severe stress overall compared with mothers, their stressor's are higher among areas of financial stability and living situations, and are comparable to rates of mother's own history of abuse and neglect.

Trend: ◄►

Page 1 of 2

100

2013 Program Report Card: Nurturing Families Network (Department of Social Services)

Quality of Life Result: All Connecticut children birth to age 9 grow up in a stable environment, safe, healthy, and ready to succeed.

Is Anyone Better Off?

Mothers participating in NFN show less rigid parenting attitudes over the first year of program services.

Figure 4. Parenting Rigidity Outcomes After 1 Year of NFN Program Participation

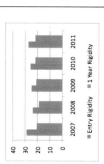

Entry Rigidity ■ 1 Year Rigidity

Story behind the baseline: Families participating in NFN home visiting show significant reductions on the rigidity subscale of the CAPI-R within 1 year of program participation. These data indicate that families have less rigid parenting attitudes and are less likely to treat their children forcefully.

Reported NFN annualized rates of maltreatment for 2005 through 2009 show that rates of substantiated abuse and neglect ranged from 4.4% (the highest) in 2007 to 1.3% (the lowest) in 2008, with 2009 rate of 2%. These rates are very low when compared with rates of 20-25% reported in studies with similarly high-risk groups that did not receive home visitation services in the state of Connecticut.

Trend: ▲

Is Anyone Better Off?

A smaller percentage of NFN children are identified as having a potential developmental delay compared to a normative population.

Figure 5. Percentage of NFN Children Identified As Having a Potential Delay on the Ages and Stages Questionnaire

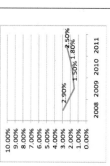

Story behind the baseline: Home visitors screen all children in the NFN program for developmental delays and social and emotional problems. In 2012 they completed 3,804 screens using the Ages and Stages Developmental Monitoring Measure. Each year only a small percentage of the children show a "red flag" for a developmental delay. The rates for the past 4 years have ranged from 1.5% to 2.9%. This compares favorably to the approximately 13% of young children nationwide who have a diagnosed developmental delay.

Trend: ▲

Trend Going in Right Direction? ▲ Yes; ▼ No; ◄► Flat/No Trend

Proposed Actions to Turn the Curve:

There have been new initiatives to serve special populations of parents. In-Home Cognitive Behavioral Therapy is offered to mothers with depression in NFN sites statewide. In addition, there are now fathering home visitors in 10 NFN sites and 11 more are being added with new federal funds. (Note: Results of a study on IHCBT will be released later in 2013. Also, the sample size of father participants for 2011 is still too small to analyze outcome data.) There is also a process study underway to better understand the services being provided to fathers. Finally, a study focusing on child outcomes is starting in February 2013. The information from these projects will help inform and improve the implementation of NFN program services and maximize outcomes for mothers, fathers and children.

Date Development Agenda:

We have developed a web-based data system, the Children's Trust Fund Data System (CTFDS), to track families and measure outcomes for families participating in Nurturing Families Network. The NFN site staff is transitioning from a paper-based system to the web-based system.

The web-based data system will save staff time now spent on the paper system and allow for the 'real time' monitoring of NFN program implementation.

Access to the most current information will enhance quality assurance and program improvement efforts.

2013 Program Report Card: Even Start Family Literacy Program (Connecticut State Department of Education)

Quality of Life Result: All Connecticut children birth to age 9 grow up in a stable environment, safe, healthy, and ready to succeed.

Contribution to the Result: Even Start contributes to the population goal and breaks the cycle of poverty and illiteracy by improving the educational opportunities of families most in need. The program provides simultaneous services to parents and their young children. It helps parents to improve their basic educational skills and become full partners in educating their children; it assists children in reaching their full potential as learners; and it assists families in moving toward self-sufficiency and out of poverty.

Program Expenditures	State Funding	Federal Funding	Other Funding	Total Funding
Actual SFY12	$479,919			$479,919
Estimated SFY13	$479,919			$479,919

Note: Federal funding for this program ended in FY 2010-11. Even Start is now funded only by the State of Connecticut.

Partners: Local adult education, federal and state-funded early and community-based early childhood programs, other state agencies such as DCF, DSS and DOL.

How Well Did We Do It? 1. Percent of children meeting standards in reading/reading readiness

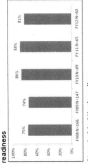

Story behind the baseline:

In FY08, six sites served 166 children; in FY12, only three sites were operational serving 60 children because federal funds were eliminated in FY11. Over the past 5 years an average of 81% of children met or exceeded standards in reading readiness for their age group (birth to kindergarten). Children participated an average of 55 hours per month in early childhood classrooms, interactive literacy activities and home based instruction. This year, over 83% of the children were infants and toddlers and were assessed every 4 months using the Ages & Stages Questionnaire (A&S). Children scoring lower on A&S were referred for further evaluation; all children referred were evaluated and children and families received appropriate services. Other assessments used for older children include: Phonological Awareness Literacy Screening, the Peabody Picture Vocabulary Test, Concepts About Print, and the Developmental Reading Assessment.

Trend: ◄► *(sustained high performance)*

How Well Did We Do It? 2. Percent of parents showing significant learning gains

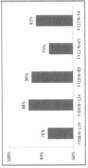

Story behind the baseline:

Over the past five years, adults in Even Start have consistently made significant gains. Every year, the program has exceeded its expected standard by more than 30 percent. The average percent of adults making significant progress during the year on their goals is 83 percent, which exceeds the overall standard for adult literacy by 40 percent or more. These are impressive gains on measures of high school completion and English language acquisition.

Trend: ◄► *(sustained high performance)*

How Well Did We Do It? Percent of parents demonstrating gains in parenting skills.

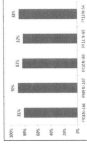

Story behind the baseline:

In the past 5 years, on average, 88 percent of the parents were determined, through home-based observations by trained observer(s) using literacy-based instruction forms, to have learned and applied parenting skills. Parents participate in parenting education classes, interactive literacy activities (with their child), and home-based instruction visits averaging 13 hours per month. Parents are encouraged to work directly with the child during interactive literacy activities and home-based instruction under the guidance of Even Start staff or collaborators. Parenting education classes are aligned with what children are learning in their early childhood classroom. Concepts underscored in parenting education are enhanced through application during interactive literacy activities and home-based instruction.

Trend: ◄► *(sustained high performance)*

Rev. 5 (12 15 12)   Trend Going in Right Direction? ▲ Yes; ▼ No; ◄► Flat/ No Trend   Page 1 of 2

2013 Program Report Card: Even Start Family Literacy Program (Connecticut State Department of Education)

Quality of Life Result: All Connecticut children birth to age 9 grow up in a stable environment, safe, healthy, and ready to succeed

How Well Did We Do It? High quality learning environments

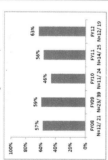

FY09 N=4 FY10 N=3 FY11 N=3 FY12 N=3

Story behind the baseline:
Infant/Toddler Environmental Rating Scale (ITERS) is a quality measure of the learning environment. An overall quality rating of 5 or higher on an ITERS indicates an environment that is 'good' to 'excellent' and benefits children in the areas of language, developmental activities, and interactions with adults and other children. Even Start sites complete the ITERS each spring.

Trend: ◄►

Is Anyone Better Off? Percent of Exiting Adults Who Attain a High School Diploma

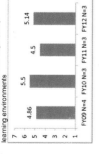

FY08   FY09   FY10   FY11   FY12
N=12/21 N=23/39 N=11/24 N=14/25 N=12/19

Story behind the baseline:
A majority of adult learners who exit the program attain a high school diploma. More than half continue on to community college or training school. Others obtain jobs in fields such as nursing (CNA), bartending, and cosmetology or start their own businesses.

Trend: ▲

Proposed Actions to Turn the Curve:
- Examine language development of parents and children using the Peabody Picture Vocabulary Test (performance measures 1, 2, 5.)
- Continue to monitor programs (state performance indicators, local evaluations, etc.), and provide professional development (performance measures 1, 2, 3.)
- Using program evaluations, deliver professional development training to help programs write literacy and social outcome goals for individual families.

Data Development Agenda:
- Align and coordinate existing data systems to ensure that Even Start's early care and education as well as adult education and training information become part of it.
- Continue to follow the same protocol of data collection on attendance and outcomes throughout each family's participation.
- Collect information on housing, employment status, DCF involvement, income and participation in other support services both at intake and at exit to determine family stability at exit.

Blank Template

2013 Program Report Card: [Insert Program Name (Insert Agency Name)]

Quality of Life Result: [Insert Result]

Contribution to the Result: [Insert Contribution]

Program Expenditures	State Funding	Federal Funding	Other Funding	Total Funding
Actual SFY 12				
Estimated SFY 13				

Partners: [Insert Partners]

How Much Did We Do?
[Insert name of measure]

[Insert Graph or Table]

Story behind the baseline:

Trend: [Use , , or]

How Well Did We Do It?
[Insert name of measure]

[Insert Graph or Table]

Story behind the baseline:

Trend: [Use , , or]

How Well Did We Do It?
[Insert name of measure]

[Insert Graph or Table]

Story behind the baseline:

Trend: [Use , , or]

Is Anyone Better Off?

Trend Going in Right Direction? ▲ Yes; No; Flat/ No Trend

Rev 5 (12 15 12)

Blank Template

2013 Program Report Card: [Insert Program Name (Insert Agency Name)]

Quality of Life Result: [Insert Result]

[Insert name of measure]

Is Anyone *Better Off?*
[Insert name of measure]

Proposed Actions to Turn the Curve:

[Insert Graph or Table]

[Insert Graph or Table]

Story behind the baseline:

Story behind the baseline:

Data Development Agenda:

Trend: [Use ▲ or ▼]

Trend: [Use ▲ or ▼]

Trend Going in Right Direction? ▲Yes; ▢ No; ▢ Flat/No Trend

Rev. 5 (12 15 12)

Appendix D

Appropriations Committee Budget Hearings

Eight Standard RBA Questions for All Programs[1]

1. *What is the quality of life result to which the program makes the most important contribution?*

This question relates to the broader mission or vision of the program. Programs are the means to an end. They are created in order to help the state achieve a certain vision or mission for improving the quality of life for people in the state (a population). For example, a job training program contributes to the result, "All Connecticut workers earn a

---

[1] This document and all other RBA resource materials for state agencies are available on the Appropriations Committee's RBA web page: http://www.cga.ct.gov/app/rba/

living wage." A waste water treatment program contributes to the result, "A clean environment for Connecticut." There is no official list of Connecticut result statements.

A result statement in its basic form can be stated as a desired result in the following sentence structure, "All (name a population) in (name a geographic location) are (statement of the quality of life condition to be achieved), e.g. "All children in Connecticut are born healthy and are developmentally on target from Birth to 3" or "All Connecticut citizens are secure and free from crime."

There may be instances where a program contributes to more than one quality of life result. Generally, you should indicate the most important of these results. If more than one result is equally important, then you may indicate the additional results as well.

2. How does the program contribute to the result?

Programs are not responsible for population results; however, they are expected to contribute to achieving one or more results. The program's statutory purpose or the purpose of the activities funded (we do these things in order to...) should be connected to the result. A program's purpose is usually narrower than the quality of life to which the program contributes. For example, the purpose of the Clean Water Fund is to encourage municipalities to treat waste water and to segregate it from storm water run-off. This program is only one element that contributes to the population result of a clean Long Island Sound. If the statutory purpose no longer seems consistent with the quality of life result you think the legislature now expects, you should explain the discrepancy.

3. Who are the programs major customers?

Customers are those served by the program. They are the direct beneficiaries of the program, the individuals, groups, or entities that receive the services, funds or other benefits of the program. For example, the customers of a preschool program are the children who attend the school and their families. Being clear about customers is essential for identifying the appropriate performance measures. The direct beneficiaries of the Clean Water Fund are the municipalities.

that apply for funding. The residents of the municipalities might be seen as the ultimate beneficiaries, but they are not the direct customers.

4. What measures do you use to tell if the program is delivering its services well?

How are you doing on the most important of those measures?

"How well" measures relate to the manner in which program activities are carried out. These measures are often referred to as process measures. Is information collected accurately? Timely? Are services delivered courteously? Efficiently? What percent of the eligible population participates in the services? Completes them? What are staff qualifications? What do customers think of the service delivery? For example, "How well" measures for the unemployment compensation program include percent of payments made within 7 days of application (timeliness) and percent of payments made without error (accuracy). "How well" measures are often related to best practices or evidence-based practices. So, if mentoring is part of an evidenced-based practice model, the percent of youth linked to a mentor could be a "how well" measure.

For the "How well" measures you consider most important, what is the current level of performance? If you have a baseline, that is data for the last 3-5 years, provide it, along with where you think performance will be in the next 2-3 years if you keep doing what you are doing.

What is the "Story behind the Baseline"? Is this baseline going in the right direction? Is it going there fast enough? What is causing the baseline to go in this direction? What are the external circumstances affecting the direction? What interactions among people or personal characteristics are affecting the direction?

If you don't have any baseline data, what are your plans for collecting the necessary data? Use the Data Development Agenda to document your plans.

5. *What measures do you use to tell if the program's customers are better off?*

How are you doing on the most important of those measures?

No matter how well you are delivering your services, how do you know if your customers are benefitting? For example, a job training program may have excellent attendance at its workshops, its instructors may all be highly qualified, and it may use a nationally recognized, evidence-based curriculum. However, we would still want to know the outcomes achieved by its customers: Did they get a job, keep that job for 6 months or a year, and earn a living wage at that job?

For the "better off" measures you consider most important, what is the current level of performance? If you have a baseline, that is data for the last 3-5 years, provide it, along with where you think performance will be in the next 2-3 years if you keep doing what you are doing.

What is the "Story behind the Baseline"? Is this baseline going in the right direction? Is it going there fast enough? What is causing the baseline to go in this direction? What are the internal and external forces affecting this performance?

If you don't have baseline data, what are your plans for collecting the necessary data? Use the Data Development Agenda to document your plans.

6. Who are the partners with a major role to play in doing better?

Government agencies alone can rarely achieve all of the outcomes that their customers desire. Partners contribute to the success of programs by making contributions to critical strategies. For example, for a program to reduce teen pregnancy, parents, teachers, doctors, clergy, and peers are all important partners. Effective strategies should include the engagement of major partners and be clear about their role.

7. *What works, what could work, to do better, or to do the least harm in a difficult financial climate?*

What are the actions that you know from the research, best practices, and your own experience are effective to "turn the curve" on the critical performance measures, that is to move performance in the right direction or prevent it from getting worse. These are the strategies that respond to the causes and forces behind the current level of performance.

8. *What specific actions do you propose to take over the next two years? Focus on 1) no-cost and low-cost actions, 2) actions to reduce the harm of budget reductions, and 3) reallocation of existing resources to obtain best results.*

To obtain the best results in this economic climate and to ensure that any budget reductions produce the least harm, what do you propose to do over the next two years? In the absence of financial resources, we need to do our best and most creative thinking, based on the analyses of the "how well" and "better off" measures, to identify no-cost or low-cost ideas, including moving funding from activities or programs that are less essential or that work less well. Be specific and concrete; focus on new actions that you will take, not what you are already doing. Remember, if you keep doing what you have been doing, you will keep getting what you have been getting.

Appendix E

RBA REPORT CARD
Program Level

DCF INTENSIVE IN-HOME CHILD AND ADOLESCENT PSYCHIATRIC SERVICES (IICAPS)
• IICAPS teams employed by contracted agencies provide home-based, family-focused, time-limited mental health services to children with severe emotional disturbances who are at risk of institutionalization
• Teams are composed of two mental health professionals (master's level clinician and bachelor's level counselor) and supervised by senior level mental health staff including a child psychiatrist
• Services are available statewide through 14 providers in 18 sites; DCF contracts with Yale University, the developer of the treatment model, for provider credentialing, training and technical assistance, and other quality assurance as well as program evaluation and reporting

Contribution: *Connecticut children grow up safe, healthy, and ready to lead successful lives.*

IICAPS improves the behavioral health of children with serious psychiatric problems while helping them to safely remain in or return to their homes from institutional care, which is key to future success in life.

Key Program Performance Measures				
	Progress	FY 09 Data (Estimates)	DCF Has Data and Regularly Analyzes	PRI Staff Analyzed
I. How *Much* Did We Do?				
1. Cases Served		1,595 total cases served, 143% more than FY 07	Yes	✓
2. Resources (DCF & Medicaid Funds)		$25.3 million, 7 times FY 05 funding level (before services were made Medicaid eligible)	Collected (by BHP); Not Analyzed	✓
II. How *Well* Did We Do It?				
3. Meeting Demand	⇨	200 average monthly wait list; 37% higher than FY 07 despite expanded capacity	Yes	✓
4. Completing Services (Planned Discharges)	=?	64% of closed cases, lower than in past but may be partly due to better data coding; wide variation across providers	Yes	✓
5. Meeting Program Standards				
a. Providers Credentialed	+	All 18 provider sites including one previously on probation meet criteria	Yes	✓
b. Fidelity to Model	+	Fidelity scores across providers have stabilized over past year; majority showing strong adherence to the service model	Yes	✓
c. Data Integrity Good	+	Data integrity scores high for all providers and average rating has risen since FY 07	Yes	✓
d. Average Service Duration of 6 Months	+	Small increase in average duration to 6.1 (5.6 in FY 07), with providers ranging from 4.5 to 7.9	Collected; analyzed for this study	✓
e. Minimum Service Intensity 5 Hours Weekly	+ =	Steady increase to average 4.4 hours since FY 07 but still below standard and varies by provider (2.8 to 6.5)	Collected; analyzed for this study	✓
6. Satisfying Clients	⇨	Parents satisfied with services across all providers every year but at slightly lower levels in FY 09 than FY 07	Collected; analyzed for this study	✓
7. Managing Provider Performance With Data	+	All provider sites meeting credentialing standards, technical assistance provided when areas in need of improvement; average fidelity and data integrity scores improving over time	Yes	✓
8. Managing Cost Per Client	?	FY 09 average Medicaid cost per case $11,585, almost double FY 07 average but are some accounting issues; much variation by provider	Not collected by DCF	✓
III. Is Anyone *Better Off?*				
9. Children Have Reduced Use of Institutional Care	+	Decreases in inpatient admissions (-37.6%), inpatient days (-45%) and ED visits (-29.4%) compared to pre-service but at smaller rates than in past; more providers with positive outcomes	Yes	✓

RBA REPORT CARD
Program Level

		on each measure in FY 09 than in FY 07		
10. Children Have Improved Functioning/ Decreased Severity	+	Increased functioning and decreased problem severity at every provider site every year (FY 07-09); performance slightly better in FY 09	Yes	✓
11. Family Functioning Has Improved	+	Improvements in average ratings better over time but variation across providers	Yes	✓
12. Children Are Free from Maltreatment	?	Analysis possible through LINK	Not collected	
13. Children Are Not Removed from Home Due to Maltreatment	?	Analysis possible through LINK	Not collected	
14. The Service is Cost-Effective	?	Cannot determine; research required	Some necessary data not available	

Story Behind Program Performance

- Making IICAPS Medicaid reimbursable greatly expanded program access, yet wait lists remain long; many area offices report waits of two weeks or more. At present there is no mechanism to centrally monitor wait times.
- Interagency partnerships with CSSD and DSS also contribute to improved access and consistent service quality for IICAPS clients. The DCF behavioral health bureau and CSSD have developed a collaborative arrangement for sharing the IICAPS service network.
- Quality assurance provided through contract with Yale appears effective, with good progress on most performance and outcome measures and strong provider accountability; significant resources (about $500,000 annually) are used to achieve this level of oversight and continuous quality improvement.
- IICAPS produces positive behavioral health results and is likely cost-effective although formal research is needed to ascertain longer term client outcomes and fiscal implications of the relationship between IICAPS and inpatient service utilization. Reasons for performance variation among providers are not clear and need to be better understood. The relationship between program fidelity and results for clients has not been fully examined to date
- While program primarily focuses on psychiatric issues, and not all clients are DCF-involved, more attention to child welfare outcomes (maltreatment, out-of-home placements due to abuse/neglect) also is needed.
- Longitudinal research could also shed light on the extent of readmissions to the program and the possible need for more supports after discharge, for example, "step down" services as some area office staff and providers suggested in PRI survey responses.
- The IICAPS program was widely praised by many providers, DCF staff, and CSSD personnel. While area office comments were generally positive, concerns were raised about quality of some teams and that newer staff seem to be lacking the experience and skills required to work successfully with DCF-involved clients.
- Providers during a PRI focus group meeting indicated it can be difficult to find treatment team personnel with the skills needed for intensive in-home services and to retain them, as the work can be quite demanding.

Actions to Turn the Curve: DCF Efforts Underway and PRI Staff Recommendations

Currently Being Undertaken by DCF:
- Arrangements have been made with DSS to share Medicaid claim data that will permit longitudinal (post discharge) analysis of behavioral health outcomes for IICAPS clients

PRI Staff Recommendations: DCF should –
1. **Require Yale to obtain feedback on provider quality from area office staff** as part of the credentialing process; ensure area office IICAPS liaisons attend program "Rounds" meetings as often as possible
2. **Calculate and track total case costs** (Medicaid, DCF, and other funding sources) to permit analysis of any trends by provider, type of client (e.g., voluntary services, juvenile justice, DCF-involved) or case severity
3. **Assist providers in recruiting and maintaining qualified IICAPS teams** through: statewide public information/education efforts (to increase awareness of the home-based team model and related employment opportunities); working directly with higher education institutions to increase the supply of trained behavioral health professionals; and continued participation in the Connecticut Workforce Collaborative on Behavioral Health
4. **Consider requiring providers to offer routine (non emergency) services on at least one weekend day a month** to increase access and better meet needs of working families

Intensive In-Home Child and Adolescent Psychiatric Services (IICAPS):
Data Development and Research Agenda
1. Collect and analyze data on readmissions; also establish a mechansim to track wait times.
2. Track child welfare outcomes (abuse/neglect reports, out-of-home placements due to maltreatment) during and following completion of treatment services for all IICAPS cases.
3. Annually review, with the assistance of Yale, variations in performance across provider sites, particularly in terms of program standards (e.g., completion rates, duration, average hours), client satisfaction, and key outcome measures to identify and share best practices; examine relationship between adherence to model and results for clients.
4. As part of longitudinal research project, develop information on supports and services children and families need to maintain improved functioning following discharge/program completion.

RBA REPORT CARD
Population Level Accountability

QUALITY OF LIFE RESULT:		

"Connecticut children grow up safe, healthy, and ready to lead successful lives."

HOW ARE WE DOING?

Key Indicators*	Progress	Most Current Data
1. Children Free from Abuse	+	• Substantiated abuse/neglect rate: 12.4 per 1,000 children in 2006 – lowest level in 10 years (high was 23.0 per 1,000 in 1997)
2. Children Born at Healthy Weight	-	• 8.2% overall low birth rate in 2006 – up from 7.4% in 2001 • Worse for Black (12.7%) and Hispanic (8.9%) babies
3. Children Proficient Readers in Third Grade	⇔	• 54.6% in 2009 – no substantial change over last few years • Worse (fewer than 30%) for students who are poor or not White
4. Children Not Living in Poverty	-	• In 2008, 12.5% under 100% federal poverty level and 26.2% under 200%, with increases in both rates since 2003 • Worse for Latino and Black children
5. High CT Social Health Index (SHI) Score	+	• 57.5 in 2006 (highest-ever level), up from 32.5 in 1997, with best SHI score = 100

* More detailed information on each key indicator is provided in Appendix C.

THE STORY BEHIND THE DATA

The state's progress in achieving this results statement for the well-being of children is mixed, with improvements in some areas (substantiated abuse, the SHI), and stagnation (reading proficiency) or drops in performance in others (low birth weight, child poverty). One consistent trend is that children who are ethnic or racial minorities persistently trail white children in each of three areas – health, education, and poverty – for which data were available by ethnicity/race.

It is important to note these key indicators are interrelated and influence each other. For example, child poverty is a factor involved in all the other indicators, while low birth weight and child abuse also influence educational achievement. A good understanding of such relationships, and how particular groups of families and children are faring, is not possible at present because state agency data systems containing client information are not linked. In Connecticut, like many other states, data sharing across agencies and service systems is impeded by confidentiality concerns and, to a lesser extent, technological challenges.

Data are lagging, by several years in some cases, and must be compiled from a variety of state and federal agencies. Except for the SHI, there is no central source of baseline and trend information on quality of life conditions for children in the state. A major data deficiency is the lack of longitudinal outcome data on children and families served by state agencies and programs that could provide insight into the long-term positive impact, if any, of various prevention, intervention, and treatment strategies.

These key indicators do not completely capture the conditions critical for positive development (e.g., stability of living environment is not directly addressed) or fully reflect major threats to a child's well-being (e.g., parental substance abuse or domestic violence). Furthermore, secondary indicators directly related to each component of the results statement are needed to better understand exactly what factors are impeding or promoting progress in terms of children's health, safety, and future success. The pilot project timeframe did not permit PRI sufficient time to identify or develop additional population-level indicator data.

The total state resources allocated to achieving this results statement account for a significant portion of the General Fund budget. A conservative estimate is that in FY 09, nearly $5.62 billion of all Connecticut state government expenditures – including about $4.45 billion from the General Fund – is devoted to promoting the well-being of children and families. This figure was developed with assistance from OFA staff, who requested this child and family expenditure information from state agencies. For agencies that did not respond within the study timeframe, PRI staff included relevant expenditure categories as outlined in the most recent OFA Budget Book.

WHAT WILL IT TAKE TO DO BETTER?

RBA Report Card
Population Level Accountability

ROLE OF STATE GOVERNMENT PARTNERS (DCF, DDS, DMHAS, DOL, DPH, DPS, DSS, SDE, COC, CTF, ECEC, OCA, JUD, CGA)

Many state government efforts to improve performance in each indicator area are underway, including:

- Child abuse: DCF is planning within the next year to launch a new intervention (Differential Response System) intended to divert at-risk families from the child protection system; the Children's Trust Fund will continue to run the Nurturing Families Network home visiting program, although at reduced funding levels; and the Commission on Children has recommended adoption of several additional strategies to prevent child abuse and neglect.

- Low birth weight: During 2008, DPH issued a report on how to eliminate ethnic disparities and launched two prevention programs: a smoking cessation program for pregnant women at several local health centers and a Sexual Violence Prevention Plan.

- Reading proficiency: SDE is focusing on closing the achievement gap and working with Priority School Districts, while the Early Childhood Cabinet has led efforts to improve pre-primary school preparation.

- Child poverty: The Connecticut Child Poverty and Prevention Council is considering economic modeling of its 12 recommendations to meet the statutory goal of reducing child poverty in the state, while the legislature's new Task Force on Children in the Recession also is working to mitigate the impact of child poverty.

To facilitate population-level accountability, PRI also recommends the following low-cost/no-cost steps be taken. They are aimed at helping state policymakers and agency managers identify where additional or modified efforts are needed to achieve desired well-being outcomes for Connecticut children.

1) The Select Committee on Children, with the assistance of the Commission on Children and OFA and OLR staff, should maintain a child and family well-being report card using the indicators listed in the above report card as a starting point. It should be used to track and report on progress made on the results statement, as well as for assessing the cumulative impact of the many legislative, executive, community, and other public initiatives undertaken with the intention of making a significant contribution to the well-being of children and families in Connecticut.

2) The legislature should mandate an initiative to bring together and share client-level results data about child and family well-being across state agencies and service systems. This effort to link state automated data systems containing critical child welfare information should be carried out by OPM, in collaboration with each of the state agency and Judicial Branch partners that contribute to the quality of life results statement developed for the PRI pilot project. OPM should build on: the data development and research activities of the Child Poverty and Prevention Council; data integration work of the Early Childhood Education Cabinet, including the mandated Early Childhood Information System underway within the state Department of Education; the Connecticut Health Information Network (CHIN) being developed through UConn; and current data interoperability projects occurring under the Mental Health Transformation Grant.

3) As part of an RBA data development agenda, the Select Committee on Children, in consultation with a working group representing the main state and non-governmental partners contributing to the results statement, by January 15, 2011, should:
   a) **identify or develop an additional key indicator of whether children are living with their families and have stability;**
   b) **develop secondary indicators for each main component of the results statement** to track progress in terms of each area of children's well-being – health, safety, and future success; and
   c) **review, at least annually, the adequacy of primary and secondary indicators** and related data resources and determine whether there may be more appropriate alternatives for monitoring how well the state is doing in achieving these desired results.

Appendix F

View live at:

www.ctkidsreportcard.org

The Connecticut Children's Report Card can be found on-line at www.ctkidsreportcard.org. This makes it accessible to legislators, government staff, non-profit leaders and other stake-holders.

Committee on Children's RBA Report Card Project

Powered By
Results
SCORECARD

CT Kids Report Card Leadership Committee

Leadership Committee Membership
Updated 10-23-2013

This group, made up of the heads of key partner agencies and organizations, provides the Committee on Children with high level executive input needed to identify and promote implementation of strategies that ensure Connecticut's young people grow up in stable environments, safe, healthy, and ready to lead successful lives. The Leadership Committee will meet quarterly to help set, steer, and monitor the state's course of action for achieving the quality of life results tracked by the CT Kids Report Card.

Mailing Address:
Children's RBA Report Card Project
Committee on Children
Room 011, Capitol Building
Hartford, CT 06106
Phone: 860-240-0370

Leadership Committee Documents

Committee on Children's RBA Report Card Project

Powered By

Results
SCORECARD

Results Statement:

The Select Committee on Children: RBA Report Card Working Group selected one result statement that encompasses what we want for all Connecticut Children: "All Connecticut Children grow up in stable environments, safe, healthy and ready to succeed.

The Committee on Children of the Connecticut legislature is building this report card on the state of the state's kids, which is required by Public Act 11-109. A wide-ranging group of people who care strongly about making things better for every child in Connecticut is helping us. We are using Results-Based Accountability (RBA), a data-based tool for getting from talk to action, to track how our children are doing and identify ways to achieve better outcomes. Ultimately, we want the CT Kids Report Card to become a guide for policy, program, and budget decisions that promote the well-being of all Connecticut children.
Our Desired Result:

All Connecticut children grow up in stable environments, safe, healthy and ready to succeed.

Right now, four key indicators related to children's health, safety, stability, and future success are highlighted on this page. Click on the icon for each domain. The arrow symbols you see at the bottom of each indicator chart show if the most recent changes are going in a positive (green) or negative (red) direction. In the future, you will be able to find many additional "headline" (or primary) and related secondary indicators about the well-being of Connecticut children on this webpage. We are still working on finding, refining, adding and explaining data. But we already know that despite our state's generally positive overall trends, when we look at results data by race, ethnicity, age, gender, income and other important characteristics, we often see a very different picture.

Our goal is to make the CT Kids Report Card website a centralized source of data that can be used by the public, as well as policymakers, service providers, and other partners, to increase accountability and transparency. Most important, we expect the report card to help the state achieve the best results possible for all Connecticut children by answering: how much are we doing; how well are we doing it; is anyone better off; and what can we do to do better?

Four Domains:

There are four domains that make up the Result Statement: Stable, Safe, Healthy and Future Success.

STABLE

The stable domain includes a number of indicators related to children growing up in a stable environment, and are reflective of three dimensions of a stable family: environment, parental engagement, and child resilience. The spotlight indicator, displayed in this report card, is the **percentage of students who are chronically absent from school.**

Click to view the details

SAFE

The safety domain includes a number of indicators related to child safety that are reflective of behaviors, life circumstances, and geography. The spotlight indicator, displayed in this report card, is the **rate of abuse and neglect for all children in Connecticut.**

Click to view the details

HEALTHY

The healthy domain includes a number of indicators related to child health that are reflective of prenatal care, medical care, nutrition, behaviors, environmental factors and behavioral health. The spotlight indicator, displayed in this report card, is the **low birth rate for single, live births in Connecticut.**

Click to view the details

FUTURE SUCCESS

The future success domain includes a number of indicators related to educational milestones, employment readiness and economic well-being. The spotlight indicator, displayed in this report card, reflects the **percentage of Connecticut third-graders who are reading at or above goal in reading, as measured by the Connecticut Mastery Test (CMT).**

Click to view the details

Committee on Children's RBA Report Card Project

Each domain has one indicator that informs whether the Result is being achieved. In the case of "Connecticut Children Grow Up in a Stable Environment," the indicator "% of Students Chronically Absent" is being tracked. In the screenshot below, you can see it has decreased in the right direction from 15.3% to 11.5% since data was first collected in 2009.

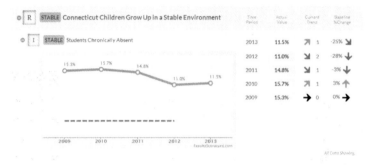

Committee on Children's RBA Report Card Project

The Children's Report Card also allows for the disagregation of indicators by race, lunch status, gender, geography, and other subpopulations

This scorecard below illustrates a disparity between Black or African American and Hispanic/Latino students in relation to other races in the State of Connecticut. Reducing this disparity has been a main focus of the Select Committee on Children.

I   **Drilldown >> Students Chronically Absent** by Race

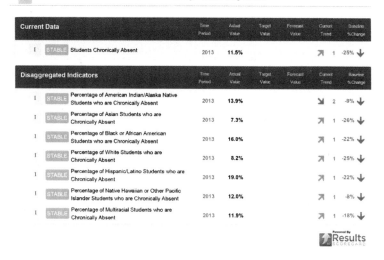

Current Data		Time Period	Actual Value	Target Value	Forecast Value	Current Trend	Baseline % Change
I STABLE Students Chronically Absent		2013	11.5%			↗ 1	-25% ↓

Disaggregated Indicators		Time Period	Actual Value	Target Value	Forecast Value	Current Trend	Baseline % Change
I STABLE Percentage of American Indian/Alaska Native Students who are Chronically Absent		2013	13.9%			↘ 2	-9% ↓
I STABLE Percentage of Asian Students who are Chronically Absent		2013	7.3%			↗ 1	-26% ↓
I STABLE Percentage of Black or African American Students who are Chronically Absent		2013	16.0%			↗ 1	-22% ↓
I STABLE Percentage of White Students who are Chronically Absent		2013	8.2%			↗ 1	-25% ↓
I STABLE Percentage of Hispanic/Latino Students who are Chronically Absent		2013	19.0%			↗ 1	-22% ↓
I STABLE Percentage of Native Hawaiian or Other Pacific Islander Students who are Chronically Absent		2013	12.0%			↗ 1	-8% ↓
I STABLE Percentage of Multiracial Students who are Chronically Absent		2013	11.9%			↗ 1	-18% ↓

Powered By
Results SCORECARD

Committee on Children's RBA Report Card Project

Viewing another subset of the data also helped us realize that students that receive free lunch are three times as likely to be chronically absent than those not eligible for free lunch.

I **Drilldown >> Students Chronically Absent by Lunch Status**

Current Data			Time Period	Actual Value	Target Value	Forecast Value	Current Trend		Baseline %Change	
I	STABLE	Students Chronically Absent	2013	11.5%			↗	1	-25%	↓

Disaggregated Indicators			Time Period	Actual Value	Target Value	Forecast Value	Current Trend		Baseline %Change	
I	STABLE	Percentage of Students Receiving Free Lunch who are Chronically Absent	2013	20.9%			↗	1	-20%	↓
I	STABLE	Percentage of Students Receiving Reduced Lunch who are Chronically Absent	2013	10.4%			↘	2	-29%	↓
I	STABLE	Percentage of Students Not Eligible for Free/Reduced Lunch who are Chronically Absent	2013	6.9%			↗	1	-28%	↓

Powered By
Results SCORECARD

Appendix G

Additional Resources for Driving the Bus

1. Friedman, Mark. *Trying Hard is Not Good Enough*. Trafford Publishing. 2005.

2. *www.raguide.org*, Results-Based Accountability(tm) Implementation Guide, Mark Friedman's website with How To Questions and Answers.

3. *www.resultsaccountability.com*, Mark Friedman's website with the latest in Results-Based Accountability(tm) news and information.

4. *www.resultsleadership.org*, Results Leadership Group website with information on consultants, trainers and facilitators that can support your quest. The following useful articles can also be found:

    a. Achieving Collective Impact with Results-Based Accountability(tm), by Deitre Epps

    b. ResultsStat Overview, by Lee, Luecking, Friedman and Boyd.

5. *www.resultsscorecard.com*: Results Scorecard is a web-based strategic management tool developed to support the Results-Based Accountability(tm) framework. It is the same tool used for the CT Children's Report Card.

Do you want to create Measurable Impact? Take the 14 element self-assessment guide found at *www.resultsleadership.org/self-assessment*. A Result Leadership Group consultant will contact you to discuss the results.

Footnotes

1 Note: There is also a set of slides on http://www.resultsaccountability.com about budget cutting using RBA, which, in a nutshell is about "least harm."

2 Youth Illicit Drug Use Prevention: DARE Long-Term Evaluations and Federal Efforts to Identify Effective Programs.

3 Project DARE: No effects at 10-year follow-up.

4 Department of Transportation.

5 Program Investigation and Review Office.